BOB UECKER feels more fortunate than most former big leaguers, because he has no feelings of frustration, of promise unfulfilled. He knows he got the most out of his talent—and it wasn't much. This is from the man whose greatest thrill in baseball was watching a guy fall out of the upper deck in Philadelphia—who loved being in the minor leagues, and who once shagged fly balls with a tuba. What he lacked in talent, Uecker made up in high jinks. His stories are hilarious, his insights keen, and his heart is as big as a diamond . . .

"An engagingly droll journeyman's view of the national pastime."

—*KIRKUS REVIEWS*

MICKEY HERSKOWITZ is a broadcaster for Houston's KPRC-TV and a nationally syndicated sports columnist.

CATCHER IN THE WRY

Bob Uecker
and Mickey Herskowitz

A JOVE BOOK

Baseball cards from the collection of Larry Fritsch, 735 Old Wausau Road, Stevens Point, WI 54481. All interior photographs not otherwise credited are from Bob Uecker's personal collection.

Cover photography provided by Lite Beer, Miller Brewing Company, Milwaukee, WI.

This Jove book contains the complete
text of the original hardcover edition.
It has been completely reset in a typeface
designed for easy reading and was printed
from new film.

CATCHER IN THE WRY

A Jove Book / published by arrangement with
the author

PRINTING HISTORY
G. P. Putnam's Sons edition / August 1982
Jove edition / May 1983
Twelfth printing / April 1987

ISBN: 0-515-09029-8

Jove Books are published by The Berkley Publishing Group,
200 Madison Avenue, New York, NY 10016.
The words "A JOVE BOOK" and the "J" with sunburst
are trademarks belonging to Jove Publications, Inc.

PRINTED IN THE UNITED STATES OF AMERICA

Acknowledgments

When people ask who made me a broadcaster, or a baseball humorist, I give them the names of a dozen pitchers in the National League.

But I also want to express my thanks to Merle Harmon, who talked me into doing an audition with ABC; to Alan (Bud) Selig, who gave me my first opportunity in broadcasting with the Brewers; and Al Hirt, for letting me try out my brand of comedy on the stage of his nightclub. I just recited the highlights of my career and the audience thought it was hilarious.

The efforts of many people went into the making of this book, but a special debt is owed to Mark Stillwell, the president (retired) of the Bob Uecker Fan Club (also retired).

To Gus, my father,
who was never surprised
when I struck out.
He would have seen the humor
in all the good it did me.

Contents

Introduction

MOST OF WHAT I have written here is true, especially those descriptions and examples of how I struggled to become a lifetime .200 hitter in the major leagues.

Some of what I have written might have happened, but didn't, and some could only have happened in the dark corners of my own imagination. I have not used any arrows, cartoon balloons or parenthetical asides to tell you which is which.

Those who love baseball as a game, the way I love it, will know the difference, and they are the ones for whom this book was written.

Preface

THIS IS BILL LEE, the rather unconventional pitcher for the Montreal Expos, on the subject of catchers:

"Catchers anticipate. They try to receive vibrations, waves. Catchers have to be very sensitive. Their attention wanders a lot. So you have to stop, shake them, get all the screws back in the right place. If my catcher wants to come out to the mound and tell me how bad I am, I'll say, 'You're right, so what shall we do about it?' I give everybody their own space."

When Bob Uecker was asked if he would like to select a friend, perhaps a former teammate, to say a few words about him and possibly provide an insight for his book, he said he would take his chances with Tim McCarver. It was an interesting choice, the obvious conclusion being that one catcher understands another. Certainly, these two do.

Uecker was McCarver's backup at St. Louis in 1964, the year the Cardinals won the pennant in a four-team pileup. Tim retired at the end of the 1980 season after a remarkable career that spanned twenty-one years. He was the first modern catcher to play for four decades, in most years a splendid performer, always a hard-nosed one.

He recalls catching a rookie lefthander named Steve Carlton in the spring of 1965, then having the young man approach him in the clubhouse and say, earnestly, "Hey, hey, you've got to call more breaking pitches when we're behind the hitter."

By then McCarver was moving into his sixth season, having established himself in the World Series as a coming star. He backed up the startled pitcher against a wall and screamed at him, "You sonofabitch! You got a lot of guts telling me that. What credentials do *you* have?"

That, as Tim describes it, was the beginning of a long and beautiful friendship, tight enough that the Phillies would bring him out of one retirement just to catch Carlton.

Between Uecker and McCarver—one catcher to another—there was never any pugnacity. When Tim became a broadcaster in Philadelphia, Bob was among his well-wishers. He knew McCarver would have to make it the hard way. There is not much comic material in a baseball career as solid as that one.

Perceptive and direct, McCarver may blow a few of the covers Uecker has created for himself, but here he is:

When I roomed with Uke in 1964, people were always saying to me, "I'll bet that's a zany room." It wasn't zany at all. You'd go down to the lobby or out to the parking lot and there'd be a string of guys telling one Uecker story after another. But he isn't one of those people who has to be *on* all the time. When he wanted to relax, he got away from people. I guess that's one of the ironies of his life. Maybe it's true of any humorist.

The thing is, you never knew what was going to come out of that imagination. Once he invented something called the Ugly Card Game. He had a friend who was a police detective in Philadelphia, who kept sending him pictures of prisoners, until he had collected fifty-two of them. We would deal them out and play a version of War. You put three cards down and one face-up. The ugliest won the hand. I was the judge in case of a tie and each guy would challenge.

There was one woman's picture in the deck. I'll never forget her. She wore a wide-brimmed hat with a feather in the back that did a kind of corkscrew. She had Coke-bottle glasses, and a half-moon scar that curled right under her nose up to one eye. She was ugly. It isn't often that you can look at someone straight on and see into their nostrils.

Uke saved that card, had it whittled down to wallet size, and would just wait for someone to come up and ask about his family. He'd say, "Doin' great. My wife just sent me a recent picture," and he'd whip out his wallet. All small talk around Uke went right down the tube.

I used to wonder at what went on in his mind. All those army sergeant routines. None of it was written down. You'd think the guy had rehearsed for years. He'd be a platoon leader, demanding to know who filled the motor pool with water. When they were thinking of making him a coach, in Atlanta, he walked around like he had a pocket watch, timing everybody. He picked up all the bullshit clichés.

He and Ray Sadecki used to broadcast the news in the clubhouse. They bought a metal frog with a key in its back, and they'd wind up the frog and have it clacking in the background. That was their tape. They'd set it up on a bench and read stories out of the paper . . . Dateline: Tel Aviv . . . and there was no way to ignore them.

I know he played for some managers who didn't understand him. I think Johnny Keane did. John was a serious man, but I think he appreciated Bob, his sense of humor.

Uke really did have some talent. The first thing you looked at was his defensive ability. His throwing arm and glove. I haven't an envious bone in my body, but I envied his arm. His relaxed, quick hands.

It's strange about catchers. They really root for each other. There isn't the kind of envy you find among pitchers. You see a guy on the mound and there is always someone in the bullpen thinking, "If he fails, I may get a shot." Catchers don't have that. I guess we got banged up too much to be jealous.

One thing about Uke, he would fight anybody. He was a docile guy, but he'd come to the front very quickly. He didn't like to call knockdown pitches, and Gene Mauch called them all the time with the Phillies. But if there was a guy you wanted next to you in a fight, it was Uecker.

Bob used to make up nicknames. He called me T-bone. He was one of those people who had a knack for immediately becoming your friend just by the way he spoke your name. T-bone. Timmy. A very affectionate thing. Not too many people are caring enough to cultivate a trait like that.

I remember listening to him talk about his dad, after his dad had his operation. It was touching, and funny. He's so comfortable that you don't feel bad laughing. Uke is so outlandish that if you missed a little, you missed a lot.

—Mickey Herskowitz

CATCHER IN THE WRY

PART I

The Bob Uecker Story

*In which a poor but honest smartass from a
small beer town in the Midwest goes off to
win fame and fortune in baseball, and is
never heard from again. . . .*

"I was the first hometown boy to sign with, and play
for, the Milwaukee Braves. Technically, I wasn't born
in Milwaukee. My folks were on an oleo run to
Chicago, and my mother was due any day. On
Highway 41, just out of town, she got the pains. My
old man swung the car off the exit ramp and she
dropped me in a mangerlike area. There were three
wise men standing under an exit light . . . one had
oleo, one carried butter, the third was a baseball
scout."

Weeks later, my mother took me off milk and fed
me beef jerky to toughen me for the Cinderella story
that was to follow.

1. A Funny Thing Happened on My Way to Cooperstown

IN JUNE AND JULY of every year I go through the same ritual—an ordeal, really—of waiting for the telephone to ring. I am waiting to be told that the dream of my lifetime has come true.

I am waiting to be told that I, Robert George Uecker, known as "Mr. Baseball" to a generation that never saw me play, have been elected to baseball's Hall of Fame.

But the call doesn't come. And I realize there is no point in getting nervous or uptight. My record speaks for itself, and the fans, at least, haven't forgotten me. I go to the Old-Timers' games now and I know I haven't lost a thing. I sit in the bullpen and let people throw garbage at me, just like in the old days.

Actually, given the way things work now in our National Pastime, and were I just a few years younger, I too could be the object of a bidding war. I would play out my option, declare myself a free agent and twenty-six teams would be drooling. I would probably have to take my phone off the hook. Can you imagine what the market would be today for a defensive catcher who had a career lifetime average of .200?

And I mean on the nose. Not .201 or .199. A cool .200, lifetime. A lot of retired players joke about being a career .200 hitter, but I was the real article. Modestly, I'd say I could command a salary today of one hundred fifty thousand dollars per annum as a backup playing sixty games. Of course, if the team I signed with was deep in catching and only needed me for thirty games, I'd be worth two hundred thousand. The fewer games they needed me for, the higher the minimum bidding would go.

Of course I'm not a few years younger, and bidding wars or not, I can't but feel a warm glow of nostalgia when I think back over my years in the big leagues. I played with three teams, in four cities, under six managers. My teammates included four Hall of Famers: Henry Aaron, Eddie Mathews, Warren Spahn, Bob Gibson.

In my heart of hearts, I believe my accomplishments were as great as theirs. What did it mean for Aaron or Mathews to hit their .350 or their forty homers? Anybody with ability can play in the big leagues. To last as long as I did with the skills I had, with the numbers I produced, was a triumph of the human spirit. I played thirteen years of pro ball, and remember all but the last six clearly. Up to the very end of my career, I was still being judged on my "potential."

Many times I have been asked how a player knows when he is washed up, through, at the end of the line. Willie Pep, the former boxing champion, once said that you could look for three signs: "First your legs go. Then your reflexes go. Then your friends go." My friends went first.

In baseball the clues were more subtle. In my case, I began to get the hint when my bubble gum card came out and there was a blank space where the picture was supposed to be. Sporting goods companies offered to pay me *not* to endorse their products. I got to the park for what the manager had announced would be a night game, and found out they'd started at 1:00 P.M. I came to bat in the bottom of the ninth, two out, the bases loaded, my team trailing by a run, and looked over at the other dugout and saw them already in their street clothes.

When a player is sold or traded, he may feel a certain rejection. But when he gets cut, well, the news is traumatic. He is face to face with that moment of final truth, that he will never put on a big league uniform again. Nor is it easy on the manager who has to break the news. How do you tell a man that his career is over, that the only life he had ever known is behind him?

I'll never forget how it happened to me. I went to spring training with Atlanta in 1968. The manager was Luman Harris. I opened the door to the clubhouse and Luman looked up and said calmly, "No visitors allowed."

I suppose it is safe to say that my sense of humor caused me to reach the big leagues at least a year late, and my sense of mischief drove me out a few years too soon. But I hung around long enough to prove that my first manager was wrong, the one who sent me back to the minors with the warning, "There is no room in this game for a clown."

There was, and is, a place for Bob Uecker, it pleases me to report. Actually, I still have the view I always had—from behind home plate. Today I'm just a few tiers

higher than field level, as a broadcaster for the Milwaukee Brewers and ABC television. I enjoy my job. It's
a lot safer up there, and I don't get booed as much as I
did when I was catching. As a matter of fact, my career
might have been prolonged if Clete Boyer had hit one
less home run in 1967.

That year a Honda dealer in Atlanta had a promotion
going at the ball park. Any player who hit a homer or
pitched a shutout in the month of September received a
free Honda. Boyer hit one the last day of the season. The
next morning I dropped by his apartment to road-test it. I
was shoeless and shirtless when I roared off down the
street in front of Clete's place.

A pack of dogs, excited by the noise, began chasing
me. Feeling for the brake, my feet got tangled, I hit the
gas instead, jumped a curb and tipped over. I was lucky
to get away with a broken right arm and a pair of badly
slashed feet.

The cast was removed three weeks before I was to
report to camp the following spring. When a trainer tried
to "work out" the adhesions by yanking and twisting my
arm, he rebroke it. My arm was back in a cast when I got
to Florida, and the Braves put me on the roster as a
player-coach.

My luck continued pretty much in that vein. One day
the club went to Orlando to play the Minnesota Twins,
and I stayed behind because of my arm. Billy Martin was
the manager of the Twins then. Billy had been with the
Braves at the end of his career, and was still friendly with
Clete Boyer and Deron Johnson. He gave them a jug of
martinis to take back on the bus. I was to meet them that
night at the Cock 'n Bull restaurant in West Palm Beach.
I had been waiting maybe a half hour when they
appeared. They were loaded when they got off the bus.

The three of us were sitting at the bar, when the next thing I knew some drunk had jerked Boyer off his stool. I spun around, got to my feet and slugged him. He skidded through the dance floor area. The bartender jumped across the bar and yelled, "Bob, dammit, no more, that's all!"

I didn't want any more problems, but as I got up a friend of the first guy hit me across the head with a full beer bottle. Busted my head wide open. When I reached up and felt the blood I thought, "Oh, jeezus." I knew it wasn't beer. Not even light beer. Beer isn't red and sticky. The wound later took forty-eight stitches to close.

A terrific fight was breaking out all around me, like a scene from a "B" western. But at that point I had one goal in life: to get the hell away from that bar. I staggered out the nearest door and found myself looking at a dead-end alley, so I had to go back in and walk the length of the place to the front door. The cops were just pulling up to the curb as I fell into my car. Jim Britton, one of our pitchers, drove me to the hospital. I had my head sewn and paid the bill, $175. I went back to my hotel room, expecting to find Boyer. He wasn't there. I called the Cock 'n Bull and whoever answered said, "Yeah, he's still here. They're both here."

The doctor had wrapped my head in one of those white bandages piled up like a turban. I put on an old fishing hat and went back to the bar. Deron and Clete were sitting right where I had left them. They were so drunk they had never moved. Deron looked up and said, "Hot damn, look who's back. Uke's here. Give us another round."

I wasn't worried about Deron. His wife was in town and she could do the worrying. But Clete was rooming with me and it was past curfew and I had to get them out of there. I finally did. I dropped off Deron at his bungalow and half-carried Clete back to the room.

The next morning my head was killing me. I felt like I had the hangover they were saving for Judas, and no matter how hard I tried, I couldn't get Boyer out of bed. At ten I went to the ball park and told Luman Harris what had happened. He said, "Okay, go back to your room and if any of the writers call tell 'em you were in a car wreck."

I finally got Clete awake and he left for the park. At one o'clock he was back. Luman had found him asleep under the stands. After the game that day, I drove to the hospital to have my bandage changed. Now the news comes over the radio: *Three Atlanta players involved in a brawl.*

A week later the Braves released me. I guess they thought I had been a bad influence, but since I was so good at getting into trouble, they offered me a job in public relations, which is how I wound up making speeches and doing the game color on television.

I am able to look back on my career now with few illusions. The highest salary I ever drew, twenty-three thousand dollars, came after my best season . . . that's right, the one in which I played the fewest games. But I had my share of thrills. Probably the biggest was when I started my first game for the Braves, in my hometown of Milwaukee, in April 1962. My folks, my friends, my old schoolmates were there. And they were all cheering.

We were playing the Giants that day and Juan Marichal was pitching. I had his bubble gum card and that told me all I wanted to know about Marichal.

Before the game. Birdie Tebbetts, our manager, said he knew a lot of my relatives were in the park, but he didn't want me to be nervous or uptight. I assured him I was fine. I had been in the minors six years waiting to get here and I was ready to play.

As I walked toward the batting cage, he hollered after me: "Kid, you're doing good, except that up here in the big leagues most of us wear our athletic supporters on the inside of our uniforms."

I hit my only home run that year—the first of fourteen in my career—off Diomedes Olivo, a forty-two-year-old rookie relief pitcher for the Pittsburgh Pirates. When the ball landed in the seats, the fan who caught it threw it back. Years later, someone turned up a tape of that home run and put together a strip for a roast-and-toast, with a staff announcer giving it the H.V. Kaltenborn treatment:

"The great power hitters of days gone by recall their first home runs in the major leagues, their eyes filled with tears and their voices shaking with excitement, every detail of their first round-tripper as clear as if it had happened yesterday. It's the same for all the great ones . . . Steve Bilko, Harry Hannebrink, Clint Courtney, big Albie Pearson, Curt Blefary and Ed Bouchee.

"And so it is for Robert Uecker. He remembers that first looping line drive and so do all his fans. Recall with us now that thrilling day when Bob stepped to the plate still looking for Number One. Here's the play-by-play, as it happened, with Earl Gillespie at the microphone:

"'. . . oh and one, the pitch swung on and a drive [voice rising] INTO DEEP LEFT FIELD . . . GOING BACK TOWARD THE WALL . . . IT MAY BE . . . IT'S BACK AT THE WALL . . . HOME RUN FOR BOB UECKER!!! Well, Bob Uecker . . . quite a thrill . . .'"

Gillespie's description was followed by five minutes of the kind of laugh track you hear at a carnival fun house, interrupted by a wailing siren and Earl's voice repeating, over and over, "Well, Bob Uecker . . ."

Actually, a home run I remember even better than my first was a grand slam I delivered a few seasons later off Ron Herbel of the San Francisco Giants. After I connected, the manager, Herman Franks, came out of their dugout to remove the pitcher, and he was carrying Herbel's suitcase. For some reason, other teams took me lightly.

If you are really going to appreciate my career—and I am not sure it can be done—I guess we should start at the beginning. I was your average hot-shot athlete in high school, an all boys school in Milwaukee. My father wanted me to learn a trade. I did. By the end of my first semester I could hot-wire a car. Baseball and basketball were my games. As a freshman I was six feet one and weighed 130, and the other guys would wear my jockstrap as a wristband.

In class, my commitment to education was less than total. I had some growing up to do, and one day it occurred to me I might get there faster in the service. What helped me reach this decision was the fact that my father spent more time at school than I did. I was a total failure. I even flunked shop. I couldn't make a bread-board. In 1954, at nineteen, I enlisted in the army.

My baseball career began there, at Fort Leonard Wood, Missouri, where they had a sign inside the post that said: *IF YOU SCREW UP IN KOREA THIS IS WHERE THEY SEND YOU*. During orientation, an officer asked if any of us had played college or pro baseball. I raised my hand. He asked where I had played, and what position. I told him I had been a catcher at Marquette, which never had a baseball team. But I figured, correctly, what could they know about Marquette?

I had pitched in sandlot ball and the Braves had scouted me two years earlier, at seventeen. I had done some catching too, and I knew the base team was going to lose its starter, Bob Schmidt, in the spring. Before being drafted, Schmidt belonged to the San Francisco Giants. Later, at Fort Belvoir, I joined a team whose shortstop was Dick Groat, who would be my teammate at St. Louis.

A friend of my father's, Louie Zimmerman, talked the Braves into scouting me as a catcher. He was the editor of a German newspaper in Milwaukee, which shows you how casual the scouting system was back then. When I got out of the army I signed with Milwaukee for a three-thousand dollar bonus. The amount bothered my father at first. We were a poor family and, frankly, he didn't have that kind of cash. Finally, he scraped it up and got me to leave home again.

For the signing ceremony, the Braves' officials took us to one of the city's swankiest restaurants. My dad was so nervous he rolled down the window and the hamburgers fell off the tray.

My dad's name was Gus. He was a tool- and diemaker from Basel, Switzerland. He was also the best man I ever knew: stubborn, funny, impatient, generous and proud.

I remember reading a story about Ernie Banks, and how his father worked and sacrificed to give Ernie the chance to play ball. His father never saw the sunlight, leaving the house before dawn and getting home after dark. When Ernie signed his first contract with the Cubs he sent a three-word telegram to his father: "WE DID IT."

I relate to that story. My father got on my ass all the

time. He never said, in front of me, that he thought I could play, and at home, listening to the games on the radio, whenever I came to bat he would turn to my mother and say, "Ach, he'll probably strike out."

But without him I would never have gotten a shot. In the minors, when I was making $250 a month and the money ran out, he was right there. He was a great mechanic and a hard worker, who never let his family— his wife, a son, and two daughters—go without the basics, even in the meanest days of the Depression. He could always make three or four dollars a day working on cars.

When I got to the Braves to stay, in 1962, he was all fired up about it. Birdie Tebbetts was the manager then and they became drinking buddies. Birdie would tell me later how he would needle my old man, saying how horseshit I was, and Gus would argue with him. By the end of the season he was second-guessing Birdie.

Gus had a fearful circulation problem in his legs, a condition that caused him endless grief. He was a big man, in his sixties, when his legs were amputated.

He had kept his troubles to himself, as he usually did. The first indication I had came from my mother, who told me he had to sleep at night in a chair with his feet on a heating pad. They were always cold. My first day back, at the end of that season, I walked into his house and made him lift his trousers and show me his legs. They were black and blue from the toes to the knee.

Had he consulted a doctor, which he had never done in his life, his legs might have been saved. But he was proud and stubborn and he suffered on his own terms.

I practically dragged him to a doctor. The examination revealed that gangrene had already set in. He was in surgery the next day. Nylon tubes were inserted in both legs to replace the veins and increase the circulation of blood.

The operation seemed a success—for one full day. I spent the night at his bedside. The next morning he started clotting. Now the doctors had no choice but to amputate. They could not even wait for my mother to return to the hospital. I was the one who had to sign the papers. Later, I was the one who had to tell him.

I don't think my father's death, a few years later, saddened me any more than the sight of him being wheeled out of the operating room, his legs gone.

He was in the hospital for twenty weeks, and my old Milwaukee teammates helped him get through the bad times. I would walk into the room and Warren Spahn or Eddie Mathews or Johnny Logan or Lew Burdette would be visiting him. My father wasn't allowed to have liquor in the room, but they would sneak in a couple of bottles and after two or three hours we would all be blasted, including my old man. The nurses could never figure out why he was so cheerful.

I came home from St. Louis the next year and he had thrown away the artificial legs the doctors had fitted to him. He was more comfortable with smaller ones, and he had rockers attached so he could shuffle along and not fall. When he had them on he looked like Toulouse-Lautrec.

The first time I walked into the house and saw him on those short legs, I just cracked up. He didn't mind, so long as I didn't cry. I couldn't stop laughing. You could push him back and forth, like a rocking toy. He loved it. We were both whacko. We had exactly the same sense of humor.

For months he stayed close to home. He was embarrassed to go into his favorite gin mill on those little legs, and he couldn't use the restroom in his wheel chair. He had to carry a jar with him. I went by the house one day, threw a jacket on him, lifted him out of the wheel chair and drove him to the tavern, the Meadow Inn. His drinking and card-playing buddies were waiting for him. He had the time of his life.

I was in Atlanta in 1968, the season after my playing career had ended, when his heart gave out. Twice I flew to Milwaukee to be with him after major attacks. I was with him in intensive care when he had what the hospitals call a Code Four. I watched the doctors restart his heart with an electric shock and by pounding his chest. In the process, they cracked a couple of his ribs.

They literally brought him back to life. A few days later, he told me he was really hacked off. He said he felt himself going, everything was soft and mellow, and suddenly everyone was beating on him.

I made my mother promise that she would take him out of the hospital as soon as he could be moved. If he was going to die, I knew he would rather it happen at home. And so he did.

He went home with strict orders not to listen to any football or baseball games on the radio or TV. Of course, he paid no attention. Gus died two months after he left the hospital, during the 1968 World Series between the Tigers and one of my old teams, the Cardinals. I knew then, if I hadn't before, how important it was to me, and to both of us, that he had been able to see me play in the big leagues.

Sure, I had my critics, people who swore I would never make it. They never bothered me. I always thought I was bigger than baseball and I think my record proves it.

2. Down on the Farm

IN OUR SOCIETY, big league has become a synonym for "first class." A friend once told me of the time Judge Roy Hofheinz was trying to get a bill passed that would allow construction of his domed stadium in Houston. As part of a public relations blitz, he flew some sixty politicians and news people out west.

They stopped off in Los Angeles to stare at an enormous hole in the ground that would become Dodger Stadium, then flew on to San Francisco, where Candlestick Park was earing completion. Everywhere they went the propaganda machine kept rolling: this was big league; that was *not* big league; this was what you had to do if you wanted to go big league.

The junket ended in Las Vegas, with dinner and a show that featured one hundred topless, statuesque showgirls. Red-eyed and hung over, the party landed in Houston just after dawn, the early morning sun all but blinding the passengers. Amid the groans and stirrings, a man named Morris Frank, known for his twangy East

Texas wit, looked out the window of the plane and saw his wife among a small crowd gathered at the ramp.

"Wal," said Morris, stretching his arms, "it sure was great seein' all them big-league boobies, but it's back to the minors today."

One way or another, I spent some of the best years of my life in the minors. I feel sorry for any ballplayer who never had to work his way up through a farm system, who never lived on sliced meat sandwiches or dressed in clubhouses where your locker consisted of a nail driven into a board. It is like going through life without ever riding on a train.

I am going to ramble a bit now, which is the way I remember the minor leagues, as a slow, rambling, breezy time in my life. I loved it, the way people dressed and talked and thought, the way they cared and didn't mind showing it.

My dad drove me to the bus station and I reported to my first spring training camp at Waycross, Georgia, to an old air force base where the Braves' lower farm clubs trained. I had just received my discharge from the service, and here I was back in the barracks.

A player who has never gone through *that* kind of camp, where the prospects numbered in the hundreds, can never really appreciate spring training. They would pin a number on your back—you might be Number 317—and each morning a crowd would collect around the bulletin board in the camp office to see who had made the Greyhound squad that day. Meaning, adios.

The signs over the toilets warned, DON'T FLUSH WHILE SHOWER IS RUNNING. This was an invitation to every guy who walked in to flush the commode and scald whoever was in the shower. You would walk out of there with a red stripe down your back.

After curfew we'd string a wire across the barracks about knee high and wait for the drunken night watchman to make his rounds. The high point was hearing his body hit the floor. Days later, when the night watchman thought he had the knee wire figured out, we would string it neck high and almost garrote him.

Ah, memories. There were no fences in the outfield, and many a player chased a deep fly ball into the high grass, spotted a snake, and came out faster than he ever went in.

If you were lucky, you might wind up with the hand-me-down uniform of your favorite big-league player. A little tape here and there and the pants would look fairly decent.

Thus prepared, I joined my first professional team, Eau Claire, in the Northern League, in the late spring of 1956. I was twenty-one, just out of the service, making $250 a month and six dollars a day on the road for meal money—just enough to keep you from gnawing on the table leg in your favorite café.

I got off to a miserable start, even for me, and at mid-season was batting just .171 with seventeen runs driven in. So the Braves had me reassigned to Boise, Idaho, in the Pioneer League, and I went on to have the kind of summer people used to have in their dreams, when summers didn't cost much.

Boise was about thirty games out of first place when I got there in July, and the Braves had sent down a whole new team in an effort to pull the club out of last place. Boise was the quintessential minor-league town.

They had an old fart who, when all the new players came in, vowed not to shave until we were in first place. By the end of the season his beard was down to his knees. The fans had what they called a Hustle Fund. If you hit a homer you got five dollars, and they passed the hat in the stands. The winning pitcher got five. A triple was worth three bucks, a double was worth two and a single got you a dollar. If you hit a homer you could stop by Pierson's Café the next morning for a free breakfast.

With all those incentives going for us, we caught fire, came from thirty games out and won the pennant on the last day of the season.

At Eau Claire, I had gone something like oh for fifty before I picked up my first hit as a pro, a grand slam homer at Warsaw. But at Boise I was hot from the start. I batted .312 and drove in forty-one runs, with thirteen homers. Lots of free bacon and eggs.

A local VIP named A. J. Archibald owned a bus line that ran junkets—by bus—to Las Vegas. They were motor homes with a toilet and card tables. When one was available he loaded it with fresh fruit and let the ball club use it on road trips, some of which covered seven hundred miles. Hell, I didn't see how they could travel in a style any fancier in the big leagues.

Our manager was a low-keyed, soft-spoken Southerner named George McQuinn, who played first base on the only St. Louis Browns team ever to reach the World Series (in 1944). In 1947, he helped bat the Yankees to the pennant, playing on the same team with Joe DiMaggio, Phil Rizzuto, Tommy Henrich, King Kong Keller and a rookie named Yogi Berra.

McQuinn never talked about his big-league career, which was just as well. When you are that low in the minors, you can't relate to the New York Yankees. We didn't know about anything outside the Pioneer League, and that was how we liked it. What we related to were the signs McQuinn posted in the clubhouse, such as the one that read:

THROUGH THESE DOORS PASS THE HUSTLING BOISE
BRAVES.

He arrived when we did, at midseason, and had just
the right touch for a bunch of eager, know-nothing kids.
He was the same, win or lose. "Now you boys," he
would drawl before every game, "you got to get out
theah and do youah job."

Every night was an anecdote. Rufus (Big Train)
Johnson was one of the three blacks on the team. He was
on first base one night during a power failure—we had
them regularly—and when the lights came back on
Rufus was standing at third, as if nothing had happened.

Boise was the kind of place where the groundskeeper
lived at the ball park, in a cabin under the stands, with
his wife and kids. He was in charge of the fireworks
display. One night he was half in the bag when he started
lighting them. After the first few, about four hundred of
them went off at the same time, knocked down the left
field fence and burned up his quarters. It was beautiful.

The ball park held three to four thousand people and
was jammed every night. It was a neat, pretty park
surrounded by mountains. Years later, when I was with
the Braves, we came back to Boise to play an exhibition
game, and the other fellows asked me about the lights,
the infield, the power alleys. I told them the place was
great, wait until you see it, a miniature Dodger Stadium.

When I got off the bus and walked into the park, I
couldn't believe my eyes. There were only about ten
light poles, and it was so dark a cat burglar would have
felt right at home. The guys really got on me.

But what I remember best about my first year in the
Pioneer League was the ball park at Missoula, Montana.
I had heard stories about a trap door behind home plate
and I thought people were bullshitting me.

Missoula was a farm club of the Washington Senators, and the fans had a theme song, "Hurry Back, Timber Jacks." We walked into the park and the players were taking batting practice, future big-leaguers like Jim Kaat, Jay Ward, Chuck Witherspoon. I saw the trap door and I still couldn't believe it.

When the starting lineups were announced, the trap door flew open and out popped the players, led by their manager, Jack McKeown, while the organist played "Hurry Back, Timber Jacks." The fans loved it, just loved it. The trap door was flush with the ground, ten feet or so behind the catcher, and once inside, you walked down a stairway that led to the home team's clubhouse.

During the game, if you had to answer nature's call, you just grinned sheepishly and made a very public exit. In most parks you walk to the end of the dugout and through a tunnel, or around a corner. Here you had to walk behind the catcher and open the trap door. Everybody knew where you were going. It was like dropping your pants.

My minor-league career took me from Boise to Wichita, Evansville, back to Eau Claire, to Atlanta, back to Boise, Atlanta again, Jacksonville, Indianapolis and Louisville. I was in more hotel rooms than the Gideon Bible.

One of our stops in the Northern League was the Grand Hotel in Fargo, North Dakota, a transient hotel right next to the railroad tracks. The steam engines hissed and whistled and tooted all through the night. The lobby was a famous gathering place for drunk Indians.

On the kind of money we made entertainment was scarce, and we killed a lot of our idle time with water fights. We would start small, filling rubbers and dropping them out the window on people walking by. Then we would graduate to buckets, balancing them on top of a door, poised to spill on the first luckless soul who entered. By the end of the night, we were taking the fire hoses off the wall and facing each other in the hallway like gunfighters. With one spray you could knock a guy clear across a room.

It was a small world and at times a silly one. But twenty-five years ago, you didn't go into pro baseball thinking you had an automatic ticket to the big time. At least, you didn't say so out loud, not if you were a hustling Boise Brave, or even a Timber Jack.

We were like guys trying to break out of a prisoner-of-war camp, knowing that every so often a lucky bastard got through. Our goal was to move up to a higher league the next season. Each move was a step closer to the Taj Mahal.

But in those days a lot of fine players with great records never got out of the minors. The times had changed. The country had changed. The people had changed. But in 1956 baseball had just begun to change. The Braves were in Milwaukee, the A's were in Kansas City, the Dodgers and Giants were heading west. There were still just sixteen cities on the big-league map, and too many players for too few teams. An infielder in the Braves' system could bat .300 for ten years in Triple-A and never stick in the majors, with Mathews, Logan or Schoendienst ahead of him.

So the minors would become his career. He would marry a local girl, get a job in the off season, and enjoy the fact that he was recognized in the community, a small-bore celebrity.

I was fortunate in the minors to have managers who guided and encouraged me and moved me along to the next rung. They were always trying to convince someone in the Braves' office that I could play, even if I was not always convinced myself.

One was Bob Coleman, a legendary manager in the minors, who had won something like twenty pennants by the time I played for him at Evansville in the Three-I League. Bob was in his sixties then, a brawny, gruff, hard-bitten guy who had the look of an old sea captain. He owned a German shepherd named Silver, and he continued the line as each dog died, so now he was up to Silver Five.

Coleman had a habit of sitting naked after a game in a beach chair, with his balls dangling between the canvas webbing, and Silver Five curled up under the chair, snapping at flies. I don't mean to be crude, but players new to the team were endlessly fascinated by that sight.

That damned dog attacked me once. We were in spring training in Waycross, Georgia, and I was warming up a pitcher when the ball got away from me and rolled past the chair where Bob was sitting, in uniform, with Silver Five at his feet. I ran toward the ball and the dog leaped on me, got his teeth into my hand and wouldn't let go. He thought I was after the old man.

With the uniforms we wore then, he could have grabbed me anywhere but the hand and not broken skin. The uniforms were all hand-me-downs from other clubs, blousy things that made most of us look like we were suffering from elephantiasis.

That down-home atmosphere was what I missed when I finally got to the big leagues. You never saw a manager with his pet German shepherd dozing under his chair, and they didn't take you out to eat on Sunday after a road game, either. Bob Coleman did.

A manager in the minors was likely to be a father

figure. And, the way it worked out, you were likely to need one.

In the 1960s the minor leagues began to shrink, some said because of television, soaring costs and competition from other sports. Today the character of the farm system has changed. You used to get a mixture of young prospects, veterans playing out the string, and ex-big-leaguers hoping for the one good streak they needed to make it back.

Now the old-timers are virtually gone. The market is for kids only. And those who don't make the majors in two, three, or four years usually return to college, or move on to something else. No more will you find a fellow spending a dozen years in the minors, beating his way from town to town.

I am not sure there would be room for a Bob Uecker in the minor leagues today, much less the majors. My brand of horseplay probably would not be tolerated, unless more talent than mine went with it.

In my last year in Triple-A ball, I almost joked myself out of the league. At midseason the Braves sent down Stan Lopata, and he took over as the regular catcher. I went out to the bullpen and began to look around for new ways to amuse myself, and my friends.

Fireworks have always been one of my weaknesses. On the Fourth of July, I talked the fellow in charge of the fireworks display into giving me one of his launching tubes and thirty boomers, those heavy-duty jobs that go off like artillery shells.

I carried them out to the bullpen and stored them, with the idea of lighting one each time we hit a homer, as a celebration. They had a fuse a foot and a half long and I wasn't sure I had the courage to light one. But that same night Neil Chrisley homered, and I put a match to the fuse and everyone in the bullpen scattered. We were hiding under benches, behind bunkers, hands over ears.

The boomer rose out of the tube with a soft poof, like a bazooka's, and just as Chrisley reached second base the thing exploded—like a sonic boom. The crowd came unglued. In the bullpen, the boys cheered.

To my surprise, the general manager liked the reaction and told me to keep it up. I continued to set off a boomer after every home run for the next few weeks.

Then John McHale, the president of the Braves, flew into town to look over the club. When he left, I was told to forget about the fireworks. The people in the homes across from the ball park had been sending telegrams to Milwaukee, complaining that the boomers were going off as late as ten o'clock at night, damned near knocking them out of bed.

For a while I thought the Braves might hold it against me. But I guess they were impressed with my team spirit. The next year I was in Milwaukee, a big-leaguer, at last.

3. Planet of the Apes

BY THE TIME I went to my first spring training camp with the Braves, in 1961, there was one thing I knew. I could make people laugh. Most rookies approach their first training camp as though they were raising the flag on Iwo Jima. Not me.

Chuck Dressen was the manager that year. At the end of camp, he sent me back to the minors with the deathless words: "There is no room in baseball for a clown."

Even though I believe he was wrong, and I believed it then, I can see how Dressen might have felt that way.

Billy Martin opened the season with the Braves, and was traded after six games. Billy was at the very end of his stormy career, and still years away from his even stormier service as a manager, during which he would be fired by the Twins, the Tigers, the Rangers and the Yankees, twice. Billy would gain immortality as the last manager ever hired by Charles O. Finley, who sold the Oakland A's some weeks later, in 1980.

Johnny Logan was another kindred spirit in that camp. He would be traded the next year and out of the big leagues in two.

The three of us were on the scrubs. In the fifth inning of those spring training games, if the Braves were losing, Dressen would send in the reserves. We would shout and jump around and pound our gloves and, in general, act as though we were being sent in to save the game. We really pissed off Dressen.

He never forgave some of us for making fun of his cooking. He considered himself a gourmet cook, and frequently prepared a large vat of chili, his specialty, for the coaches, the writers, and his guests. He never offered any to the players.

For this and reasons less worthy, we would slyly drop cigarette butts, matches, and sand from the butt box into the chili when Dressen wasn't watching. Later, we would sit there and watch the VIPs eat that mess and laugh ourselves right out of the room.

I heard that the quality of Dressen's chili remained high the rest of the season, but the team didn't perform so well. He was fired with twenty-five games left and Birdie Tebbetts replaced him.

That year, 1961, would be the last full season I would spend in the minors. I batted .309 with fourteen homers at Louisville, and when I reported to the Braves the next spring I felt almost as though I belonged.

I would be hailed as the first Milwaukee native to play for the Braves. Later, I would be hailed as the first Milwaukee native to be traded by the Braves. Hometown boy makes good.

When I joined them the Braves were a fifth-place team going nowhere. Del Crandall was the starting catcher and a great one. I appeared in just thirty-three games and batted .250—just right, not high enough to raise their hopes or low enough to cut my pay. I woke up to a new world every day, thrilled to be in the big leagues, grateful to be around people I had heard and read about for years. But it was tough to be a young catcher working with a veteran pitching staff.

One day I went out to the mound to talk to Lew Burdette, after a couple of runners had reached base. When I got there, he said, "What the hell do you want?"

I said, "Nothing. I just came out to give you a break."

Lew said, "Don't be coming out here. I don't want you out here. They"—and he waved his gloved hand at the crowd—"think you're giving me advice. And the only thing you know about pitching is that you can't hit it."

My reaction was to go back behind the plate and tell the hitter what pitches were coming. I understood Lew's position.

Still, my stay with the Braves was not without a splash of reflected glory. I was on the receiving end of the game that made Warren Spahn the winningest left-handed pitcher of all time. Spahn was a joy to watch, a master craftsman. Some nights I would catch him without using signs. He didn't have the big breaking ball. Spahnie had a popping fast ball, screwball, and slider. If he wanted to pitch inside to a right-handed batter the pitch was always going to be a fast ball or slider. If he wanted to pitch away, it was going to be a fast ball or screwball.

The only sign I gave him was *in* or *out*. I'd just put up the mitt as a target. He would mouth the words: "Where do you want it?" And I'd mouth back: "In the web."

You can do that when you win and, in those days, Spahn nearly always won.

But overall the Braves had declined from their World

Series years, '57 and '58, and had become the one thing baseball fans can't accept. A mediocre team. Not good enough to compete, not bad enough to be lovable.

I would go on to sit on the bench for a lot of losing teams. Fans often asked me how the players were able to stay up, stay ready, when it was August and the sun was blazing and your team was out of the race?

I can only answer for myself. I would just go out and get likkered up. Same way under pressure. Just go to the bottle. The game is easy when you go out there and play it straight. But when you take half a jug of V.O. and toss it down, you make the game a challenge. I used to get a big kick out of someone coming up to me after a game and asking about a certain play, and I couldn't remember it.

In my day, which was before the age of the mega-bucks, these were the little things that held the players together. I do concede that the players are better behaved today. Chewing tobacco was more popular in my time. You would get dressed and walk onto the field in your clean, white, sanitary socks, with your shoes shined, and somebody would come up and drop a bad wad right on your ankle. Seemed like it was always just before the gum card people were going to take your picture. (Some habits are hard to outgrow. I admit it: I still chew. Even on airplanes.)

The funny thing is, people never believed me when I told them it didn't bother me if I didn't get to play. In the darkest, most insecure corner of my soul, it didn't. I always figured the more I played, the closer I was to going back to the minors.

For years, whatever reputation I had as a player was based entirely on my label as a "good defensive catcher who only needs a chance to play," and on my ability to hit . . . Sandy Koufax.

Koufax? *That* Sandy Koufax? Right. I hit him. I hit him hard. Neither one of us ever figured out why. But whenever Sandy is interviewed about the hitters who were tough on him, he always mentions my name. And he usually gets a laugh, even though he means it.

One night, with Koufax on the mound, the Dodgers gave me an intentional walk to load the bases and bring up the pitcher. Tom Gorman was the umpire and John Roseboro was catching. As I tossed the bat toward the dugout, I turned to the two of them and said, "Boy, if this ever gets out you guys are going to get a letter from the commissioner."

It was obvious I was not going to catch much in Milwaukee. Behind Crandall they had a fine young rookie coming up in Joe Torre. I would be gone from Milwaukee in 1964. (The Braves would be gone in 1966, bound for Atlanta.)

They did me what turned out to be a great kindness. The Braves traded me to a St. Louis team that was going to put on a terrific stretch kick and win the pennant in the National League. The season would be two-thirds gone before anyone knew the Cardinals were in the race— including the Cardinals.

My immediate role seemed to be to provide another character for the clubhouse act developed by Tim McCarver and Ray Sadecki. They had worked up a number of zany routines, inspired by the popular Jackie Gleason show, with Tim as Crazy Guggenheim and Sadecki as Joe the Bartender.

The movie *Planet of the Apes* would not be released until four years later, but in 1964 the two of them were ahead of their time. They went out and purchased gorilla masks. They wore them everywhere. On the plane, on the bus, in the clubhouse, sitting around naked in their hotel room. Believe me, many a maid went tearing out of their room, towels and bedsheets flying.

Some nights they would take a suit coat and trousers and concoct a dummy, stuffing it with sheets and pillows. Then they would arrange the clothing just so, put the mask on top and stick a cigar in his mouth and prop him up in one of those big, overstuffed chairs. Now, their room might be ten floors above mine, but they would carry that creation down the stairwell at four o'clock in the morning and knock on my door. I would get out of bed, stumble to the door, and there would be this ape, with a cigar in his mouth, sitting in a chair in the hall.

As a near legend among the fringe players of my time, I was a natural choice to be commissioner of the Batting Practice League, formed among the pitchers and reserves in St. Louis. We actually played a game every day. We chose up teams and had lineup cards. Even as the team was clawing the Phillies and Reds in the real pennant race, we were holding our own.

We used to get to the park early for the BPL. There was a lot of money involved. Ron Taylor was the captain of one team and Sadecki captained the other. As commissioner, I also had to pitch batting practice. One day, Ron Taylor's team hit out of turn. Sadecki let them bat and then, as the rules require, called it to my attention.

I walked off the mound to get Taylor's lineup card, and when he saw me coming he ate it. I mean, as I got within a few feet he yanked the card out of his pocket, stuffed it into his mouth, chewed gamely and then swallowed the pieces. It was better than a spy movie.

Afterward, Sadecki insisted we follow Taylor around

until he went to the toilet and passed the lineup card, so I could rule on whether his team had batted out of turn.

I drew the line at this indignity, but on the scrubs the craziness went on day in and day out. At the end of the year we awarded the trophies.

All in all, the '64 Cardinals were the perfect team for a player whose personality demanded expression. There was talent on the field, intrigue in the front office and madness in the clubhouse. We were curiously untouched by the pressures of a pennant race. We did not even know we were in one until September. This was the loosest, goosiest team ever to come from ten games behind to reach the World Series, a drive in which Robert George Uecker played his own, as shall be seen, crucial part.

PART II

Inside Baseball

In which he reveals that if an athlete works hard, stays in shape, never gives up, and hits .200, he can attract one of the funniest fan clubs anyone ever had.

"There were a great many people who thought that the Cards had made a mistake, trading two ballplayers for one Uecker. As the season wore on, Uecker proved that they were indeed correct . . ."

4. The Fan Club

THE STORY YOU are about to read is true. The names have not been changed to protect anybody, innocent or not, on the theory that if I'm willing to use mine so should they.

Some years ago the zaniest and most unlikely fan club in the annals of baseball was formed. The story behind it is the stuff of legend. How it came to be, the spirit and purpose of the club, the tenacity with which its hero was supported, would melt the heart of a Greek statue.

In 1964, a student at Drury College in Missouri, Mark Stillwell, and his brother, Paul, noticed that the St. Louis Cardinals had not won a game in which I had played from the start of the season until the second of July. This record struck them as worth celebrating, and they did so in what I thought was a commendable and logical way.

They organized The Bob Uecker Fan Club.

In four years the club attracted over five hundred members (names and addresses are on file with the club president, as well as the FBI and the CIA). Sweatshirts bearing my name and likeness were manufactured. An official matchbook was printed, a slogan adopted ("Bob Uecker is a Great American"). Attempts to plan an appreciation day had to be postponed, either because I kept getting traded or because the school cafeteria was not available.

It is hard to say what forces came together to start such a movement. I suppose it was a natural reaction to the pressures of the Vietnam War. Those were turbulent years.

Mark Stillwell was a clean-cut, otherwise normal college type, the sports editor of the Drury *Mirror.* We kept in touch during his undergraduate days, and later when he served in the navy. Eventually he returned to Drury as the school's director of sports information.

I don't think I ever met more than three or four club members at a time. Every so often one of them would show up at whatever ball park my team happened to be in, and if I played that day the news would soon be all over the campus. They would report back with all the excitement of a bird watcher sighting a gray-speckled spanarkel. "He went oh for three," they would say, breathlessly, or, "he chased a ball all the way to the backstop."

When Mickey Mantle retired, he began receiving scrapbooks kept by his fans throughout the country, more than fifty of them. Sometimes late at night he would take one out and thumb through it. "It gave me goose bumps," he said, "to know I had that kind of effect on people."

My first reaction to hearing that I had a fan club was to say nothing, and to lie low for about two weeks, until I could see if Ray Sadecki or Tim McCarver was behind it. There came a day when I received in the mail from Mark the scrapbook the club had maintained, in three or four volumes. Turning the pages, my entire career flashed before my eyes. It was a little like drowning.

The tone was set with the introduction, a little defensive, I thought, like a lawyer appealing to have a guilty verdict overturned. To quote Mark Stillwell, "This book is an attempt to present the case of Bob Uecker. Sometimes it is straightforward, sometimes it is biased against Bob Uecker and, mainly, it is biased in favor of Bob Uecker."

Now I like that approach. I am reminded of the vacuum cleaner salesman who knocks on a customer's door and says, "Let me give you the pros and cons of this product."

Mark goes on: "It was the kind of sudden impulse thing I couldn't explain, and this hurt my presentation. But my heart was soon fully in it and my enthusiasm won me a lot of support.

"This (scrapbook) tells it all. The pictures and words vividly record the course of the Bob Uecker Fan Club and the successes and failures of Bob Uecker. (It) is all collected here, and this is probably the greatest conglomeration of Bob Uecker data ever assembled anywhere."

The casual fan may feel that the kid was taking a lot for granted, not knowing what they might have had on file at, say, the British Museum. But when I first read that paragraph, I could envision the scrapbook being made into a television docu-drama, the highlights of my career in baseball: Bob Uecker getting on a plane to start a road trip; Bob Uecker sleeping on a plane; Bob Uecker getting off a plane.

The club caught on. Where all the members came from I never knew. I am not sure I wanted to know. I was told that several were under ten years of age. The oldest was ninety-two.

By the time the club was organized, I had spent nine years in organized ball—two of them in the majors—and had made fifteen moves to ten different cities.

As a big-leaguer, I had appeared in eighty-six games, with forty-one hits in 186 times at bats for an average of .220. I had scored sixteen runs and driven in fourteen, with five doubles and two homers—all in less than three seasons.

Jeez, no wonder I had my own fan club.

Mark Stillwell took special note of one part of my game: "There is a lot said about Bob Uecker's speed. Most everybody generally agrees that he is one of the slowest runners in the game. He had a race with Dick Groat in spring training to see who was the slowest on the team and Groat outran him. The fact also stands out that Uecker has stolen six bases in his career. All, however, before 1960, and all in the minor leagues. He swiped one base at Eau Claire in 1956 and two at Boise the same year. He got two more at Boise in 1958 and one at Jacksonville in 1959. And that's it."

This, I think, came under the heading of what the boys called "some of the good stuff" they had learned about my career.

Another item from early in the scrapbook: "Paul saw Uecker play in a minor league game at San Diego in July of 1963 against San Diego. Uecker played for Denver. He batted sixth and grounded out twice and walked as Denver lost, 3-0. His name had been left off the scoreboard and the box score in the San Diego paper the next day spelled his name 'Uekcer.'"

When the Braves traded me to the Cardinals only a few days before the start of the 1964 season, getting catcher Jim Coker and outfielder Gary Kolb in return, I was just another journeyman ballplayer. Although manager Johnny Keane announced that I had been obtained to back up Tim McCarver, and "make our catching solid," I did not instantly capture the hearts of the people of St. Louis. As the president of my own fan club would later observe: "There were a great many people who thought that the Cards made a great mistake, trading two ballplayers for one Uecker. As the season wore on, Uecker proved that they were indeed correct. He fielded like a slow, wounded turtle behind the plate. He ran like a batting cage with a flat tire, and he hit like he didn't know what the word meant. He cost the Cards some ballgames with poor throwing and hit into double plays or made outs at key spots. His batting average dwindled to the .200 mark. He became the butt of some jokes and his very presence in the lineup gave the Cards a defeatist attitude. He seemed to be a loser like the Cards hadn't had since the days of Dal Maxvill. He became the scapegoat. People began to blame things on Uecker. And Uecker deserved every bit of it."

At this point, you might conclude that the fans were not yet solidly behind me. No matter how poorly things were going for me, no one made excuses. They told it like it was with a bluntness that would have made Howard Cosell weep.

The diary of the 1964 season went on: "Johnny Keane constantly used pinch hitters for him and never played him unless McCarver was about to drop and it was the second game of a doubleheader and the team was on the road and the Cards were facing a lefthander.

"Uecker went from bad to worse to terrible. It seemed that the Cards just couldn't win with him in the lineup. Through the first three months of the season, the Cards lost every single game in which Uecker's name appeared

in the box score. No matter what he did, it never
failed . . . when he played, the Cards lost."

Some athletes can't handle compliments and are
embarrassed by praise. Thank the Lord I'm not one of
them. My patience paid off.

"On July 2, 1964, baseball history was made in
County Stadium in Milwaukee. The St. Louis Cardinals
won a game in which Bob Uecker played. Of course, he
didn't play the whole game. That would be expecting a
little too much. Uecker, whose true talent was probably
revealed when he won a cow-milking contest in Houston, has given Harry Caray what is probably another
good omen, and the Cardinal announcer values such
things.

"He caught three innings and the Cards maintained a
4-3 lead and finally won a game with him in the lineup.
He was rushed to a hospital for immediate observation.
Cardinal fans across the country postponed plans for the
biggest event of the year in St. Louis, Bob Uecker Night,
at which they intended to assassinate him.

"Uecker entered the game in the seventh. The Cards,
thanks to Julian Javier's second homer in two games and
tenth of the year, and a couple of pinch hits, had tied the
Braves, 3-3. The Braves brought in Hank Fischer to
pitch. Since Johnny Keane had unwisely batted for
McCarver, he had no other catcher. It is not unwise in
itself to bat for McCarver, but the thing is that when you
do you have to use Bob Uecker behind the plate. So,
when Fischer came in to pitch to Flood, who should
come riding in on the golf cart with him but Uecker, to
catch the seventh, eighth, and ninth. (The fans) shud-
dered. Another game lost, they figured. Flood walked
and Brock hit a sacrifice fly to center to give St. Louis a
4-3 lead.

"In the bottom of the seventh, Bob Humphreys walked the frst man he faced and sent him to second on a wild pitch. Same old Humphreys, we all thought. Then, Humphreys proceeded to retire the next nine men in a row to save Ray Sadecki's ninth victory of the season. He even struck out two men. When Uecker batted, of course, he was called out on strikes. Typical. The only reason the Cards won is that nobody, with the possible exception of Humphreys, knew that it was Uecker behind the plate."

The Uecker jinx had been broken. And a strange coincidence took place. The Cardinals caught fire. Cautiously, Keane tried me again. In a game at Pittsburgh I went hitless in five trips, but the Cards collected twenty hits and breezed, 12-5. The same week I caught again, and we rallied for eleven runs in the eighth innng to win, 15-7.

There was magic in the air. I refer to the scrapbook: "Four nights later, Uecker actually got a base hit. His batting average had dwindled to .173 and he boosted it to .179. On the twenty-fifth of July, he caught a full game. He came to the plate five times. He had three walks and two singles, scoring twice. He caught an excellent game and even got several closeup shots on national television when he *got hit in the neck by a foul tip*.

"He now had twelve hits in twenty games and his average was back around the .200 mark. He has four runs for the season and two runs batted in. Clearly, he intends to play a better brand of baseball for the rest of the season than he started with. . . . As Harry Caray said this afternoon, 'This is the catcher we traded for.'"

Blissfully unaware of the activity stirring on my behalf, I found myself blending into what had become, surprisingly, a pennant-contending team. At midsummer, the rumors were buzzing around the league that Johnny Keane was finished in St. Louis, to be replaced at the end of the season by Leo Durocher.

But, suddenly, the Cardinals had begun to make a charge at the leaders. On the last day of August, we beat the Braves, 5-4, to pull within a couple of games of the second-place Reds. The Phillies seemed uncatchable, but as Yogi Berra once said, "It's never over until it's over." My single in the last of the ninth drove in the winning run to beat the Braves. We had rallied from four runs down, and earlier I had hit my first homer of the season off Denny Lemaster. The crowd went berserk. I had the spirit. So did my fan club, which I still did not know existed.

In Springfield, the kids at Drury College were taking credit for turning around the pennant race. On the day the Bob Uecker Fan Club was started, the Cardinals were a game under .500 with forty-seven wns and forty-eight losses. Since then we had won thirty and lost thirteen, a .697 pace. No doubt about it. The formation of the club had coincided with the revival of the Cardinals as a factor in the pennant race. It was almost metaphysical.

Their "strange impulse" had undergone a change in character. The club was still a put-on—hey, my kind of game—but no longer a put-*down*.

I was soon to meet my two truest believers. On September tenth, with the Reds in town, the Stillwell brothers drove to St. Louis and arrived at Busch Stadium, wearing their designer sweatshirts and armed with their membership list and a carton of matchbooks. Mark recorded the scene: "I watched Uecker for a while as he sat in the dugout comparing hands with Ken Boyer, and then he came out to play catch with his faithful friend, Bob Skinner. There were several kids in the front row of the box seats looking for autographs as Paul and I boldly walked down into an area which is no-man's-land for autograph hunters because of the nasty attitude of the ushers."

They had not been at the railing long when the printing on their sweatshirts caught my eye. I left Skinner and walked over to investigate, a little wary, my grin getting wider as I drew closer. Mark made the introductions and said, proudly, "I'll bet you didn't know you had a fan club with one hundred seventy-six members down in Springfield, did you?"

I laughed out loud. "No," I said, "I sure as hell didn't. You aren't the ones who have been booing me, are you?"

They assured me they were not. I signed a team picture and two scorecards, and Mark gave me a personalized Bob Uecker matchbook. I stuck it in my back pocket and went off to catch infield practice.

Mark continued his observations: "Happily, I went back to my seat to watch the Cards do battle with the Reds. Uecker caught the first game (of two) and reached base on an error in the second inning. Ken Boyer hit a towering two-run homer in the third to give the Cards the lead, and the first hit off Gibson was a line drive by Deron Johnson in the fourth into the left-field seats. Uecker grounded solidly into a double play in the fourth and bounced out in the seventh. He was on deck in the ninth when McCarver got the game-winning hit. The Cards won, 3-2.

"As I walked into the park I had been confronted by a teenager in civilian clothes talking to a scorecard vendor. I recognized him as Bob Baker, the Cardinal batboy. He said, pointing to my shirt, 'How many of youse are there?' I told him, one hundred seventy-six. 'Where are you from?' he asked. I told him Springfield. He asked if we were all boys. No, I replied, we do have some girls.

"All day people would look at my sweatshirt and either snicker, or come right out and laugh or make some smart comment or wisecrack. It was almost as if nobody ever heard of Bob Uecker and none of them ever appreciated him.

"However, it was late in the second game when I saw a sign above the Cardinals' bullpen in left field that read BOB UECKER ALL STAR. (There was another sign in front of the hot-dog stand in the left-field bleachers that said ED SPEZIO FAN CLUB.)

"Lou Brock homered in the first, McCarver homered in the seventh and Flood singled in Javier in the ninth with what was the winning run in a 3-2 victory that tied the Cards and Reds for second place.

"Later, we were walking up Sullivan Avenue and a young lady in a car saw my sweatshirt, leaned out the window and said, 'I agree.' I turned around, astonished, and yelled, 'Hey, a real Bob Uecker fan.'

"We decided to go to Stan Musial's restaurant to eat, but they told us we couldn't come in with that kind of attire. They were rather nasty about the whole thing, I thought. Maybe I should have had a McCarver sweatshirt on. We finally wound up eating at the old standby way out on Chippewa, at Chuck-a-Burger."

End of a perfect day.

The boys went back to the campus to push their membership drive with new vigor. I didn't *really* take it seriously, but, what the heck, in the weeks since the club was founded the Cardinals had swept from seventh place to second. Lay that secret handshake on me.

I am not the kind of player who lived by batting average alone. And I do feel that I made a contribution to the team's pennant charge, if only by helping to maintain the morale of the club. Actually, I won two or three games with clutch base hits, but there is no point in going into all the details. It gets to be too much like walking through a garden, admiring the roses, and saying over and over, "Here's another beauty."

Actually, I was getting my share of playing time. On September thirteenth, I was behind the plate when we became the first team since 1923 to score in every inning. We pounded the Cubs, 15-2, racking up eighteen hits—off six Chicago pitchers—and taking advantage of seven errors. Curt Simmons got the win, his fifteenth of the season. At Drury College, the club members said the game was a tribute to my greatness.

A moving team has a grace all its own. The Cardinals could do nothing wrong in September, winning twenty-one of twenty-nine games, and squeezing past the Reds and the Phillies in one of the wildest of all pennant races.

The Cardinals had approached the season with a huge question mark. Stan Musial, one of the game's legendary hitters, their spiritual leader—and left fielder—had retired. A spot in the lineup that had not required a second thought in twenty years was suddenly wide open.

Four players were tried there as the club limped through the season's early weeks. Just before the All-Star break, a trade with Chicago brought in Lou Brock, in return for pitcher Ernie Broglio. The deal was not a popular one in the locker room. Ernie had been a proven winner, and was one of the few players who never failed to laugh at our skits. Not much was known of Brock, a young outfielder with speed, a slight build and a newsboy's innocent face.

After a slow start, Lou began to run and hit. Left field ceased to be a problem. In another trade, Roger Craig arrived to help Barney Schultz in the bullpen, and Bob Gibson found his control and got hot.

Of course, there was another, less obvious factor. I suppose some people will feel that my quoting from the scrapbook, at this point, is merely a device I can hide behind to appear modest, to avoid saying things that sound self-serving. The best way to answer that charge is to quote from the scrapbook: "On July 26, 1964, the Bob Uecker Fan Club came into existence and was an immediate and lasting success. We of the club don't pretend to take complete credit for the events which occurred in the city of St. Louis and which culminated on the afternoon of October fourth when the St. Louis Cardinals became the National League champions. However, we do point to the record and will continue to point to it as long as skepticism to our cause appears.

"One quiet fact stands out. Prior to the time the Bob Uecker Fan Club was formed, the Cardinals were in seventh place. After that, they won forty-six and lost only twenty-one and rolled past team after team until they had moved into the National League throne room. They then defeated the New York Yankees to win the World Series.

"We don don't claim that *we* won the pennant. We don't claim that Bob Uecker won the pennant. And we don't claim that the Bob Uecker Fan Club won the pennant. We simply point to the record before and after the formation of the Bob Uecker Fan Club!"

Credit aside, I enjoyed the race as both a player and a spectator. In what has become one of the more celebrated collapses in all of baseball lore, the Phillies blew a lead of six and a half games with twelve games to play. "It was like watching someone drown," said Gene Mauch, the manager.

Gus Triandos, the big Greek catcher, called it "the year of the blue snow."

Meanwhile, the Reds were gallantly trying to win the pennant for their manager, Fred Hutchinson, who was dying of cancer, and who gave up the team to Dick Sisler in August. Sisler was called the "acting manager," a phrase with a reassuring temporary ring to it. But the Reds would never again jump to the orders of Fred Hutchinson. He knew it and they knew it. He died in November.

For the Cardinals, the finish was not without its bittersweet moments. The club at one point won eight in a row, five over the Pirates, to leap past the Phillies and Reds into first place.

The race went down to its final weekend, whereupon the Mets almost ruined it for us. The Mets. The lowly, comic-book Mets. They beat us in the first two games. They were like cockroaches. It wasn't what they ate or carried off, it was what they fell into and ruined. We still needed a win to clinch the pennant, and Gibson delivered on the final day.

So the Cardinals surprised not only the Phillies, the Reds, and the experts. They surprised the Cardinal ownership. Bing Devine, the team's general manager, and Johnny Keane's closest friend, had been fired in August, with the club trailing in third place. The papers were saying that the manager's job had been offered to Leo Durocher. Keane kept his silence.

Now here were the Cardinals, meeting the New York Yankees in the World Series. Mantle, Ford, Skowron and Howard. Naturally, the Series went the distance, and Bob Gibson beat the Yankees in the seventh game, on two days' rest, starting because, in the words of Johnny Keane, "I had a commitment to his heart."

As Jack Benny might have said, "W-e-l-l-l-l." Do you think the Cardinals's owners were red-faced when Keane's team turned around and won both the pennant and the World Series? Hastily, they broke off talks with Durocher. Keane was offered a new contract, with a respectable raise.

John was in the sweetly ironic position of being able to tell them to take their offer and stick it in a beer can. Which he did. In a startling postscript to the Series, the losing team fired its manager, Yogi Berra, and replaced him with the manager of the winning team, Johnny Keane. Sadly, he joined the Yankees in time to catch them on a downward slide, and was fired in 1966, proving again that in baseball, as in politics, there are no final victories.

According to my calculations, in my six years in the majors I did not play in 675 games, not counting All-Star games. A lot of the games I did not play in were big games, historic games—involving names like Stan Musial, Willie Mays, Roberto Clemente, Henry Aaron, Frank Robinson; two or three no-hitters, marathons that lasted eighteen or twenty innings, things like that.

Looking back over my entire career, I am proudest of the World Series I did not play in for the Cardinals in '64. Tim McCarver caught every inning of every game.

For the Series, McCarver batted .478, scored four runs, drove in five and even stole a base. In all sincerity, I doubt that I could have improved on his performance.

But in all modesty, I can say that I probably received as much publicity as any fellow could for not playing in a World Series. Before the first-game ceremonies in St. Louis, I was on the field shagging flies with the rest of the scrubs. All the players were using gloves except me.

I was wearing a tuba. That probably requires an explanation.

There were four Dixieland bands on the field that day to entertain the crowd before the game. When the band in the left-field corner took a break, I noticed a tuba sitting there, looking neglected.

So I whipped it on and started catching fly balls with it. I didn't catch them all. A few, possibly several, hit the rim. The Cardinals later received a bill from the tuba player, wanting to be reimbursed for the damages. I had to kick in for it.

The Series turned out well, and that was as close as I came to getting into it, so you would have to say the money was well spent.

5. The Best Defensive Catcher in the League

MY LAURELS MAY be the only thing I never rested on in my career, and I know my fans felt the same way. By way of a preamble to the 1965 season, the fan club recorded this touching thought: "Last year our goal was to get one member for each point in Bob Uecker's batting average. A late spurt gave him a .198 average, leaving us slightly short . . ."

That spring of 1965, coming off the championship season, I found myself with the kind of opportunity second-stringers dream about and seldom get. Tim McCarver broke a finger toward the end of camp and was out of action opening day and longer. I figured to get a chance to catch every day.

Now being a second-stringer is just about the most awkward role in sports. You have to accept the fact that the only way you will see any substantial action is for the fellow ahead of you to get hurt. If it happens, you have to be ready, but you can't appear too eager or too pleased. I mean, you can't go up to Tim McCarver every day and ask, "How's the finger?"

Red Schoendienst had succeeded Johnny Keane as manager of the Cardinals, and every day I read in the papers how he wasn't worried by the thought of having to go with Uecker. "He'll get better with more work," said Red.

Of course, this went contrary to my own theory, which was that the less I played the more likely I was to stay in the big leagues. But I prepared myself to take the risk. At least once in your life, you have to gamble. I had a heckuva spring, hitting over .300 and even banging a couple of homers.

I was the starting catcher on opening day of 1965, with Bob Gibson on the mound, when the defending champion Cardinals met the Chicago Cubs at Wrigley Field. It was just another typical day in the life of Mr. Baseball, meaning that:

—The game was called on account of darkness at the end of eleven innings with the score tied, 10-10;

—The Cards scored five runs in the top of the first and Gibson, one of the great pitchers of his day, couldn't hold the lead;

—I tried to steal home in the fifth inning and was out at the plate . . . I thought the sign had been flashed for the suicide squeeze bunt, but apparently it hadn't. I was sorry about that;

—I drew a walk with the bases loaded in the first inning to drive in a run;

—In the sixth I crashed into the field boxes chasing a pop foul and badly bruised my left kneecap. There went my career as a temporary regular catcher. The Cards had to press into service Dave Ricketts, a utility man who had been signed two days before as an insurance move.

The omens were not good. My personal historian, Mark Stillwell, took note of the crisis: "The St. Louis Cardinals won the 1964 pennant with a furious stretch drive. Then they won the World Series. With the same team looking much improved, they were picked by many to win again in 1965. But they started badly, losing five of their first six games and eight of their first twelve. Clearly, action was called for as something had to be done to pick the team up. Something *big* was needed. The Bob Uecker Fan Club moved in and stemmed the tide."

Mark and three other members of the club, Joe Fisher, Mike McCloskey, and Mike Wright, arranged to be in St. Louis on Friday night, April 30, to watch a four-game, weekend series against the Pirates. I was not in the lineup as we won the first two games, both by scores of 3-2.

On Sunday, the boys got to the ball park early: "Uecker was standing out in front of the left field wall. Eventually he wandered in and went into the dugout. When the team came back out, he started playing catch with Boyer and Carl Warwick. McCloskey had a poster that had Uecker's picture on it and I yelled at Uecker and held it up for him to see. A broad grin crossed his face. Shortly he came over and I took some pictures of him. I asked him if he was going to catch one of the games and he said he was. After the dugout interview, I got the attention of Cardinal announcer Harry Caray. I handed him a clipping from the Drury *Mirror* (the student paper) and he started reading it eagerly with a smile on his face. He asked me if he could keep it. I was only too glad to oblige.

"Then the game started. Donn Clendenon and Willie Stargell homered off Gibson in the first to put the Pirates ahead, 2-0. Then, in the bottom of the first, it happened. At roughly 1:25 P.M., Harry Caray uttered those immortal words: 'Members of the Bob Uecker Fan Club are here today, hee hee, from Drury College.' Short, simple, and to the point."

I didn't play in the first game as the Cards came back to win, 9-5. Mark continues: "Then came the big second game. Uecker's moment of glory . . . The Pirates had used sloppy Cardinal fielding and a general clobbering of Bob Purkey to get three runs and there were still men on first and second with two out in the third and Del Crandall at bat. He drilled a single to left and Jerry Lynch came charging around from second.

"Lou Brock fielded the ball in left and threw toward home. It wasn't a particularly strong or impressive throw at all. Uecker had to go several feet into foul territory away from the baseline to get the ball as Lynch barreled down the line toward home. At the last instant, Uecker grabbed the throw on one hop and lunged at Lynch. He stretched himself out horizontally and just managed to tag Lynch on the shins. Lynch bowled him over and Uecker quickly bounced up with the ball clenched tightly in his fist. The umpire raised his right arm high. The crowd roared. I was the loudest.

"In the lower third he got to bat. A wild cheer came up from our section after the play he had made to end the top of the third. Then he hit a long fly into right that had us all on our feet. Bill Virdon ran a long way and finally caught up with the ball on the warning track in front of the wall.

"Bob Veale was tough for the Pirates. As the bottom of the eighth rolled along, Veale was breezing, 4-1. He had given up just one hit (a homer by Ken Boyer) and fanned nine. Then came his downfall. Bob Uecker stepped to the plate.

"With grace and poise, Uecker took a ball in the dirt. Crandall said something to the umpire as he picked up the ball and through my field glasses I could see Uecker grinning out of the side of his mouth. He carefully watched the second pitch go high. We were pulling for him now, vocally, and I think the people around us sensed it as they kept turning around. The next pitch came in and was again low. Ball three! One more and we had a base runner. Veale wound up. He fired. It was inside! Uecker trotted down to first base as the four of us gave him a standing ovation. Veale had faltered. Just to make things exciting, he threw over to first to try and get Uecker. (Imagine Uecker trying to steal.)

"That brought up Phil Gagliano to bat for Barney Schultz. The crowd was up and hungry for a rally. We were up, too, yelling to Gagliano for a hit and warning Uecker not to get picked off. Uecker is one of the slowest men in the league. The danger of his scoring on a triple by Gagliano was only slight.

"Gagliano amazed everybody as he lined a shot off the right-field wall. Uecker took off for second base. The ball bounded away from the right fielder as McCloskey took a picture of Uecker lumbering along and we all cheered wildly in an effort to give him more speed. The ball bounced into the bullpen and the pitchers there scattered. It rolled under the bench and the right fielder chased it there and picked up the bench and looked for the ball and then kicked it away and had to run after it again.

"By this time Uecker had reached second base and was getting a little tired and had to slow down from the brisk pace he had been setting. The right fielder located the ball, but tripped over the pitching rubber in the bullpen and fell headlong out on the grass. The ball kept rolling away. Uecker was digging for third, but was obviously laboring. The right fielder picked up the ball and fumbled it a couple of times and let loose a weak throw that rolled into the second baseman, who also fumbled it. Uecker started his slide. The second baseman dropped the ball and picked it up and threw toward third and it was another weak throw. The ball bounced in the dust and caromed off the third baseman's forearm and into the waiting arms of the pitcher who also bobbled it before he picked it up and flipped it back to the third baseman, who tried to put the tag on the sliding Uecker. The play was close. He was safe!

"It was at this point that Joe Fisher remarked, 'He looked like he was goin' up a forty-five-percent grade.' By now we were all ecstatic that Uecker had started a rally that might conceivably change the course of the ballgame. Curt Flood came up and promptly singled to left and in a blaze of speed, coming from a second wind, Uecker roared home with his second run of the season to make it 4-2. There was loud shouting in our box and shaking of hands as our boy finally got off the base paths and into the dugout. McCloskey grabbed my arm and pointed to the scoreboard. 'That run up there belongs to Uecker,' he shouted at me.

"Then Lou Brock singled and Gagliano came in to make it 4-3. Groat bounced into a double play, but Flood scored to tie it up. Boyer lined out to the shortstop to end the eighth. We went wild, as the game was tied. And Veale had been taken out.

"In the bottom of the ninth, Bill White led off against Al McBean. All he had to do now was homer and the Cards would win. He hit the second pitch into the right-field pavilion for a 5-4 win. The Cards had won four straight from the Pirates and had reached the .500 mark for the season, and had climbed in three days from tenth in the National League to a tie for fourth.

"The boys had come through in the clutch. And Uecker was in the center of it all. As Joe remarked to me in the three-run rally in the eighth, 'He broke it open.' There was a woman in front of us who was enjoying our antics as much as she was the game. She turned around and looked at me and said, 'You're right! Uecker did it.' And then she turned to her husband and I heard her say, 'I never heard of Bob Uecker in my life until today.'"

I see that game, that rally, and that remark as a microcosm of my life. I guess it would be easy for some people to say that anyone's career could sound exciting if you described every pitch of it. On the other hand, perhaps not.

I am not trying to make a big deal of the fact that I drew a walk and scored the run that got us back into a rather meaningless game in May. Someone had to get us started. Nor do I care to say where that play ranks among all the most unforgettable plays of my career. That would be like trying to single out your favorite noodle at a spaghetti dinner. But out of that narrative, the line that appeals to me most is, *"Uecker started his slide."* The line has a kind of melancholy ring to it.

The season rocked along. McCarver and I were still nagged by injuries, but we struggled to stay in the lineup. A few days later, I hit my first home run of the season, but it went to waste. The Giants scored five runs in the top of the tenth inning to break a tie and beat us, 10-5. It was a weird inning, and I figured in it in a prominent way.

We had Ray Washburn on the mound. There were
runners at first and third with one out when Ed Bailey, a
backup catcher who was even slower then me, batted for
the San Francisco pitcher. He swung at an 0-2 pitch and
rapped a grounder toward Phil Gagliano at second base.
The perfect double play mix: crisp ground ball, slow
runner.

Phil charged the ball and juggled it. Then he picked it
up, decided he had no chance to get two, and fired a
strike to home.

The only problem was, I wasn't there. The ball almost
hit the plate umpire in the gut. I had headed down the
first-base line. If Gagliano fielded the ball cleanly, I
needed to back up the relay to first. Meanwhile, the
winning run scored and the Giants went on to get four
more.

After the game, Bob Broeg, the veteran St. Louis
baseball writer, bumped into Tom Sheehan, the round,
red-faced Giants' scout who always reminded me of a
house detective. Broeg told Sheehan that, man and boy,
he had been watching the Cardinals for forty years and
had never seen that play.

"No," boomed Sheehan, in his big, bass voice, "and
man and boy, I'll bet you've never seen many catchers,
either, whose last name begins with the letter *U*."

As the 1965 season unfolded, it developed that
beneath the clown's mask, inside my bench-warmer's
shell, beat the heart of a semi-regular and might-have-
been .300 hitter. I darned near blew my image.

In May, Red Schoendienst decided to platoon me with
Tim McCarver. I started twelve games. We won eight of
them. That month the Cardinals made their best and last

bid to move into first place, pulling to within a game and a half of the Dodgers.

My fan club began to suspect that they had created a monster. On May fifth I cracked my first homer of the season, against the Giants. Three nights later, I started rallies with a walk and a single, and kept the Phillies from scoring the winning run in the ninth by tagging out Alex Johnson on a close play at the plate. Over the radio network, Harry Caray exulted: "How Uecker ever held that ball I'll never know."

Like monks recording their daily prayers, my scribes committed every word to the club scrapbook.

May 16—"Uecker had a hit to raise his average forty points to .190. Jack Buck spoke for all of us when he said, 'Uecker has been really stinging the ball, but it just isn't falling in.'"

May 17—". . . threw out two runners attempting to steal, was the middle man on a double play and blocked the plate to keep the Phillies from scoring. Harry Caray called his arm 'phenomenal.'"

May 20—". . . had a hit and scored run as Bob Gibson won his eighth, 12-2."

May 21—". . . laced a single to center in the fourth, with a 2-2 count and the tying run on second, to drive in his third run of the year and raise his average to .214 (the highest it has been in some time). Two innings later he walked. It seems as if every time Uecker catches, he walks once. Never twice, but always once, except Thursday when he was hit by a pitch. He obviously has a good eye at the plate."

It is dangerous for an athlete to believe his own publicity, good or bad. I never believed mine, partly because I never read any until after I had retired. But for a fleeting moment there, in 1965, I was getting very good ink indeed.

In late May, we beat the Dodgers twice to cut their lead to one and a half games. I collected two hits off Claude Osteen and two—of course!—off Sandy Koufax, one a double that just missed being a homer.

I was only in the lineup against left-handers, which meant that I could look forward to a parade of people named Koufax, Bob Veale, Chris Short, Bo Belinsky, Dick Ellsworth, Al Jackson, Jim O'Toole and Claude Osteen. I had to adopt a new philosophy. I learned to dread one day at a time.

The win over Koufax turned out to be the high point of our season. I scored the winning run and lifted my average to .286, at the time the third highest on the club, behind Curt Flood and Lou Brock. We should have known right then that the Cardinals were in trouble.

Out last hurrah came in Los Angeles, on July 25, when we beat the Dodgers in ten innings, 3-2, before a crowd of fifty thousand. As luck would have it—I am trying to be humble about this—I had two hits off Koufax, one a homer. Poor Sandy. He was the greatest pitcher of his time, and whenever I stepped in to face him he didn't know whether to laugh or to cry.

After that we went right down the tubes. The Giants swept a three-game series from us at home, and by the first week in August we were just over .500 and out of the race. Typical of the way the season had gone, McCarver and I went on the injury list at the same time, just as we had in April. Once more Mike Shannon was yanked from the outfield to fill in as the emergency catcher. Tim had a spiked left thumb. I had a split right thumb. Between us we had a complete set.

Sometimes there is no way to explain why a championship team takes a pratfall. Some call it the Fat Cat syndrome. But the Cardinals had to fight too hard in 1964, won too late and by too little, to be complacent. True, we had changed managers, but Red was a clone of Johnny Keane: a good man, quiet, serious, diligent, with the same way of handling a team.

We had virtually the same lineup that had won the World Series. Yet at the point where we had begun our pennant drive the year before, our tank was empty. Injuries nagged us. Simmons and Sadecki won fifteen fewer games. Boyer, White, Flood, and Brock saw their averages drop between twenty and forty points. When the locusts come, they devour everything.

During this period I made an interesting discovery. These were all players with high standards, which they had set for themselves. When they failed to meet them, the fans and the management came down hard. I had no such problem.

I found myself a more frequent guest on Harry Caray's postgame radio show, reserved for The Star of the Game. I appeared in September after a win over the Mets, during which I picked a runner off second and singled off the shortstop's glove. The hit at first had been called an error.

Harry asked me if some players didn't worry a lot about whether balls were called hits or errors.

"Some players," I admitted, "will get on first base and reach down and pick up a handful of dirt and when nobody is looking, they'll glance up at the scoreboard."

Harry said, "What do you do when it's a close call?"

I said, "I reach down and pick up a handful of dirt and when nobody is looking, I glance up at the scoreboard."

"I guess you like to see them call it a hit."

"Well, I always like to count 'em as a hit myself," I

replied. "I count everything—hits, walks, fielder's choices, everything. If I hit the ball good, I count it."

Harry asked, "Well, by your own system, what are you hitting right now?"

"Six-forty-three," I said.

There was not a lot to laugh or cheer about by the time the Cardinals ended the season at home. We stood in front of the dugout while Lou Brock received a plaque at home plate for breaking the club record with sixty stolen bases. Without turning my head, I whispered to McCarver, "If I had been in the lineup every day that could be me out there."

I did, in fact, have my best season in the majors. I played in fifty-three games, batted 145 times, with thirty-three hits, seventeen runs, seven doubles, two homers and ten runs batted in—all career highs. I hit a hard .228.

I was the catcher when Roy McMillan, of the Mets, stepped in the batter's box to start his two thousandth game. When Sandy Koufax set the National League record for strikeouts in a season, 349, I was the hitter he fanned to tie the record.

Over the years we had a great personal rivalry, Koufax and I. Thank the Lord I didn't destroy the boy's confidence.

Although the Cardinals had tumbled to seventh place, I had performed reasonably well as a spot starter. No one would blame me for the decline. No one had said, "As Uecker goes, so go the Cards." I felt secure. I even thought I might get a small raise.

What I got was a trade to the Philadelphia Phillies, along with Dick Groat and Bill White. In return, the

Cardinals received pitcher Art Mahaffey, outfielder Alex Johnson and catcher Pat Corrales.

The news broke on October 27, 1965, on the heels of a trade that sent Ken Boyer to the Mets. The fan club felt betrayed and outraged. The kids stopped just short of asking the president to double the guard at Pearl Harbor.

Mark Stillwell took the news harder than I did: "To trade Bill White after the job he has done is in itself a crime against humanity. To trade Dick Groat might be partly understandable, much as the Boyer trade was. But to trade Uecker was the unkindest cut of all. This is an unpardonable sin. And, when you don't get anything for him in return, it's doubly bad.

"Myra Becker called me over in English and told me the Cards had traded Bob Uecker. I almost fainted. I called Dave Schulty down at the newspaper office and he confirmed the report. Never in my life had I been so sick about something. Joe Fisher almost keeled over when I told him. I can't in any way rationalize trading White, and I can't even stomach trading Uecker.

"The first thing I did was to write a story for the Drury *Mirror,* letting the world know that the Bob Uecker Fan Club will not desert its hero in his time of great need. Then I prepared to write a nasty letter to Bob Howsam, the general manager of the Cardinals, who perpetrated this great crime."

Howsam was not popular with the players, although I hasten to add that being popular with the players is not essential to being a general manager. At times, it isn't even desirable. But Howsam had replaced Bing Devine, who had spent his life with the St. Louis franchise and was widely admired for his fairness.

Howsam was no amateur. He had a long family history in sports, and had set minor-league attendance records in

Denver. He was a large, affable man, with a round face and a high, soft voice. He sounded a little like Liberace. He liked to dash off memos and post clippings on the bulletin board in the clubhouse, and the players are suspicious of anyone who makes them read things.

What Howsam had done was to follow an old and honored custom. It is called cutting the payroll. Baseball teams prefer to rebuild with younger players, especially those with low overheads. Boyer, Groat and White drew hefty salaries. I was thrown in, I think, just to confuse people.

A pained and angry letter from Mark Stillwell poured into the Cardinal offices the day after the trade:

Dear Mr. Howsam,

I've been a Cardinal fan for a long time and I don't know when anything has happened that has disappointed me and disgusted me so much as the trade just completed with the Philadelphia Phillies.

In Bill White, the Cardinals had the best defensive first baseman in the National League, and also one of the most dangerous power hitters around. In Dick Groat they had a smart, steady ballplayer who knew more about the game than most shortstops ever learn. In Bob Uecker, they had the best defensive catcher in the league and one of the strongest throwing arms in baseball. These are three men I would seriously doubt that the Cardinals could afford to (lose) unless they obtained some outstanding talent in return.

In Art Mahaffey, we've picked up a discontented pitcher who won just two games. Pat Corrales has good minor-league credentials, but not overly impressive. Alex Johnson may be the sleeper in the deal, but he'll have to hit more than eight home runs to help the Cards.

If Red Schoendienst doesn't get an ulcer trying to decide what he has left when he gets to St. Petersburg next spring, I'll be surprised. But, while you're at the trading game, see if you can clear up some of this sadness by unloading part of this horde of pitchers that has piled up and come up with a bona fide power hitter.

> Yours truly,
> Mark Stillwell
> President
> Bob Uecker Fan Club

Nowhere, this side of politics, do people get madder, or choose up sides faster, than in baseball. A single trade can disrupt the pace of an entire city. People honk their horns. They are rude to each other in elevators. Children wet their beds.

We lost some of this emotional outpouring when the free-agent traffic began. When a player sells himself on the auction block, and his team gets little or nothing in return, the fans can't argue about which side got the better of the deal, or wonder how the front office could be so stupid. As a former player, I have mixed feelings about free agency. It is like coed housing in college. We are shocked and confused, and we ask why didn't it happen twenty years ago?

Howsam's answer to Mark was stock front-office stuff, soft-answer-turneth-away-wrath:

Dear Mr. Stillwell,

Thank you for your letter of October 27 regarding the recent trade.

Naturally, it is never pleasant to trade ballplayers that have played such good baseball for the club and were so popular. But in order to try to keep our ball club strong and in contention, it is necessary to make changes.

When a trade is negotiated, it is the thinking of the entire Cardinal organization. Our manager is consulted, our scouts are consulted, because they are the ones who thoroughly check the records and actually watch the various players throughout the year; our minor-league department is consulted to find out what they know about the player or players involved. I could never be part of trading a player on the spur of the moment. A lot of research goes into the players we receive in a trade and also into a player before we trade him. We feel we have made trades which will be beneficial to the Cardinals.

I appreciate your interest, and thank you for taking the time to write to me. We hope you will have the opportunity to see many games in the new stadium next year.

Kindest regards,
Bob Howsam
General Manager

In other words, they were not going to call off the trade. Uecker was going to Philadelphia, a town where, on Easter, they boo the little kids who don't find eggs.

6. Uecker's Last Hurrah

THE PHILLIES, like the Cardinals, were a team trying to regroup. No manager had survived more adversity than Gene Mauch. His first team had established a major-league record by losing twenty-three straight games in 1961. Near the end of the streak, they came off a road trip to find a large crowd waiting for them at the airport in Philadelphia. They figured, obviously, it was a lynch mob. A pitcher named Frank Sullivan called out, "leave the plane in single file. That way they can't get us with one burst."

But the fans came to welcome them home again, to cheer, to give them support. There is no way to know what makes a Phillies fan tick. They rallied behind Gene Mauch, and in time he gave them a contender, only to see the Phillies blow a ten-game lead in the nightmare season of 1964. The next year they were never a factor, and now Mauch had decided to retool the club.

I felt at home with the Phillies, when I reported to camp at Clearwater in March. The roster included such cashews as Richie Allen, who liked everything about a ball park except getting there; Bo Belinsky, the flamboyant left-hander who thought he had been Rudolph Valentino in a prior life, and John Boozer, a pitcher whose idea of fun was to eat bugs and worms and watch people gag. He did a better job in the clubhouse than D-Con. He would be talking to a writer and one of the players would hand him a live worm or a beetle. Some of the reactions were terrific.

Belinsky reported to camp two days late, explaining that he had been trapped by a snowstorm in Texas on the drive from California. Those Texas snowstorms can be murder.

In addition to the ex-Cardinal trio, Mauch had traded for Phil Linz, an infielder the Yankees had fired for playing the harmonica on the team bus after a loss, and Jackie Brandt, who once watched part of an All-Star Game while sitting in the dugout in the nude.

The Phillies had a terrific roster. I don't mean in talent, but in names, the kind that headline writers loved, like Wine and Boozer, and the kind that just had a certain ring, like Ferguson Jenkins, Cookie Rojas and Clay Dalrymple.

I had been brought in to back up Dalrymple, a seven-year vet and an underrated fellow, whose .213 average in 1965 was well below his form. Clay hit from the left side, which meant that once again I would have a chance to start against the left-handers. It was hard to tell if I had made any progress. I had been traded to my third team in three years. The Phillies issued me uniform Number 10. I had worn 9 in St. Louis and 8 in Milwaukee. Was this progress?

When the players talked about the best and the brightest managers, the name of Gene Mauch often came up. He was quick-tempered, but he did not give up on people easily. His career as a player had been similar to mine. He was a shortstop who always seemed to line up behind someone better, such as Phil Rizzuto, with the Yankees, or Pee Wee Reese, with the Dodgers.

Frustrated, still a kid, Mauch once confronted his manager, Casey Stengel, in the dining room of a hotel where the Yankees stayed. "Dammit, Casey," he blurted, "I've got to play."

Stengel looked up from his soup and nodded. "Go talk to Mr. Rizzuto," the old man said. "If it's okay with him, it's okay with me."

Mauch was the most intense manager I ever knew. He would sit on the bench with his arms folded and his eyes never stopped moving. He didn't miss a thing. They used to tell a story about when Mauch was playing for the Red Sox, and on the way to the airport the team bus got stuck under an overpass. The driver and the team got out to study the problem. Finally, Mauch said, "Let the air out of the tires and fill them up on the other side." And so they did.

I was in the lineup on opening day, 1966, caught Chris Short and drove in a run with a single as we beat the Reds and Joe Nuxhall, 3-1. Then a really uncharacteristic thing happened. I hit home runs on consecutive days at the end of April. In my first six games, I had produced four hits, half of them homers, and driven in six runs. A curious start, it was worth three stars and a full, hand-lettered page in the scrapbook:

TWO HOMERS
IN TWO
DAYS!

BIG UKE
IS STARTING TO
FIND THE RANGE

ONLY 505 CAREER
HOMERS BEHIND
MAYS & OTT!!

Ah, yes, the future stretched ahead as smooth and inviting as the Pennsylvania Turnpike. When I connected for my third homer on Memorial Day, against the Mets, Mark wrote a story for the school paper at Drury, and mailed a copy to Bob Howsam. The Cardinals were in the process of sending Mahaffey and Johnson to the minors. The trade was looking rather one-sided for the Phillies.

The story went like this: "Bob Howsam has finally, publicly, admitted in May that he was completely wrong in October. The story we got then was that we were trading White, Groat, and Uecker for Johnson, Corrales, and Mahaffey because we (the Cardinals) were fully committed to our youth movement.

"Well, it doesn't look too good for smiling Bob. How can you say you're in a youth movement and trade a thirty-one-year-old slugger like White and then keep a broken-down, thirty-seven-year-old pitcher named Curt Simmons, who only pitches against the Phillies and can't beat them?

"With his homer, double, and three runs batted in on Memorial Day, and his two singles two days later, Uecker raised his average to a lusty .266. With three homers . . . he seems likely to get a new career high in every hitting department, and last year had been his best. He's hitting better than either Bill White or Dick Groat, the men he was traded with, and that ought to make him the big man in the deal. The key man in the deal!

"Howsam, you're an idiot."

With aplomb, Howsam wrote back:

Dear Mr. Stillwell,

Thank you for sending along the article which appeared at Drury.

It's nice to know, too, that you have remained Cardinal fans.

We hope you and your Fan Club will have the opportunity to visit the new Busch Memorial Stadium and see the Cardinals play. I think you'll enjoy it.

> Kindest regards,
> Bob Howsam
> General Manager

The first time the teams met in 1966, the Phillies edged the Cards, 5-3. Bill White singled home our first two runs. I singled to open the winning rally and scored the tie-breaking run on a bases-loaded walk to Groat, who had two hits. It's true, hitting well is the best revenge.

On June 3, I slugged my fourth homer of the year, equaling the total for my entire big-league career. The blow was off an ex-teammate, Ray Sadecki, then pitching for the Giants. By the All-Star break I had raised my total to six, the same number as John Callison, a guy who was usually good for twenty-five to thirty a season.

I would have felt great, except that everybody around the Phillies kept wondering what was wrong with Callison. Four teams figured to stay in the pennant race most of the way, the Dodgers, Giants, Pirates, and the Phillies. We needed a big year from Callison. In fact, we needed a big year from everybody.

The point should be made right here that it can be harmful for a fellow who doesn't hit homers to suddenly start banging a few. It is like a guy who discovers girls late in life and thinks he can catch up all at once. And the next thing you know, you are in a jar at the Harvard Medical School.

But sooner or later you have to try. You see a Richie Allen twitch a muscle and the ball flies off the bat and lands five hundred feet away. And you think, is there any reason I can't do that? The next thing you know, your hands are down at the end of the bat and all your weight is on your heels.

In a way, those homers, hitting in the .270's, and getting four (4) votes for the All-Star Game may have been my undoing. Up to then my theories had stood the test of time, like milk of magnesia: 1) The more I played, the closer I was to getting shipped out, and 2) the better I performed, the more they expected.

If I had been content to just hit .200 every year, all singles, and throw out a runner now and then, I might have played as long as Gaylord Perry. Your body doesn't wear out very fast when you catch a game every four or five days.

On July 17, I tagged my seventh homer in what turned out to be a fifteen-inning win over the first-place Giants. On the Phillies, only Allen and Bill White had more, even though a total of twelve players had started more games.

I had no personal goals in mind, which was just as well because I did not hit another homer during the rest of the season.

We stayed in the race until September, then became the first of the four contenders to fade. Chris Short won twenty games and Jim Bunning finished with nineteen. A late-season slump by Bill White was costly, but he drove in 103 runs and popped twenty-two homers.

Seasons that end badly tend to blur, a series of pitches half-forgotten at the moment they are half-missed, in games that are half-played. But it was a thrill, that year, to watch Richie Allen, young and untamed, blossom into a superstar. He hit forty home runs and fought Hank Aaron for the title down to the final days. He drove in 110 runs and batted .317. And he was going to get stronger and better. He would in time overpower this game and, unfortunately, himself.

Allen was one of baseball's new talents, a prodigious long-ball hitter. He preferred horses and cars to the company of people, but he was seldom loud or rude. He asked only to be treated like a man. In view of what Richie accomplished, the request did not seem unreasonable.

Part of his problem was that no matter how much he accomplished, it was never enough to satisfy all of his critics. Some just didn't like him, his color, his style, his habits. Others simply felt that he didn't get the most out of his huge gifts. Many a time, on his way to the plate, Richie would tell us he was going to take two strikes and see if he could hit one pitch. He would do this against some of the best pitchers in the league. He drove Gene Mauch wild, but more often than not he came through. He was just that good.

Richie did not take direction well, he was careless about the time, and he liked to sip the cooking sherry. We would get in the back of the plane, glowing slightly, and sing harmony, all the old barbershop songs. We were a happy pair.

I was a witness to the events that led to Richie's famous car-pushing accident, which left him with a mangled hand. Someone had given him an old stock car. He had it at the ball park one day, and he invited Dick Groat, Bob Skinner and myself to ride back to the Presidential Apartments with him. On the way, he tried to show us how to speed shift a stock car, and going from first to second he jammed the gears into reverse. The gears locked. We pushed the jalopy over to the side of the road and that was where it stayed, until Richie had it towed to his apartment.

I don't know how long the car stayed there, but at last he decided to move it. He tried to push the car from the front and his hand slipped and went through the headlight. From then on his hand was like a claw, after the surgeons did what they could to repair the tendons. After that I called him "Crash" Allen. A lesser man would have been finished. Richie regained the use of his hand and played ten more stormy seasons.

My own season was a deceptive one, as my seasons sometimes were. In the final weeks my average shrank to .208. But I had almost as many runs batted in (thirty) as I did base hits (forty-three). I saw the most action of my career, catching seventy-six games and playing one inning at third base, although I no longer remember why. It probably had to do with whatever strategy Gene Mauch was using that night.

I figured I had done well enough to go another year, and that was as far as I ever planned. Big-league baseball players, as a group, fool no one but themselves. We are like Oskar in *The Tin Drum*, the little boy who would not grow up.

My fan club was growing older. It had somehow acquired 476 members, and the hard cord were now seniors preparing to graduate. We were bonded, in a curious kind of way. They were like having your own private gag, my Pookah, my Harvey the Rabbit made real. They redeemed my view of life; that the world belongs to those who know when to laugh at it. I am not sure what they got in return, other than a hero without the trimmings, a hero who could never let them down.

Well, almost.

At midseason, Mark had made the following entry in the scrapbook: "Since 1966 will probably be the last really active year of the Bob Uecker Fan Club, it seems significant that we should set a definite goal for ourselves. It would be altogether fitting and proper for the Phillies to get into the World Series and for Uecker to be the hero, but we have a much simpler goal.

"We want Uecker to either hit a triple or steal a base. He has never done either in his five-year career in the big leagues and we think it's high time for one or the other . . . We realize he isn't fast, but a determined man ought to be able to accomplish these things.

"He may not know how we feel about this. I ought to write and tell him."

Which he did. To no avail. Another year without a triple or a stolen base.

I continued to hear from the club. They had subscribed to the Philadelphia *Inquirer*. They had mailed a check to the Phillies for a yearbook and team pictures that as yet were undelivered, and they were thinking about setting fire to Connie Mack Stadium.

That winter I received a funny-serious letter from Mark:

Dear Bob,

   The second volume of the Bob Uecker Story is all
but complete and it looks like it's going to be every
bit as good as the first. We had a lot of material to
work with this year, largely because you came
through with your best season. I only got to see one
game, a Monday night affair at Pittsburgh late in
August, but you delivered a key, run-scoring single.

   The Cardinal fans discovered something this
year. When you were traded for Corrales, we went
from two catchers to one and your friend McCarver
had a fine year but he had to play 150 games and
that's a few too many. I think that is one trade that
will go down in the books as a disaster for St.
Louis. Now that Charlie Smith is gone, I'll see if
we can't figure a way to get you back and let you
play third base. . . .

   I'll be graduating from Drury next May along
with my number-one sidekick, so we won't have as
much time for active fan-clubbing. The Navy has
plans to send us somewhere for three years, but I'll
get to St. Louis before July and catch some Phillie-
Cardinal games. We're all hoping you'll turn in
another fine year in 1967!

                         Sincerely,
                         Mark Stillwell
                         President
                         Bob Uecker Fan Club

   The reference to Charlie Smith is worth noting now.
The Cardinals traded Smith that winter to the Yankees in
return for Roger Maris, who had chased Babe Ruth's
ghost across the summer of 1961. It was an even trade,

one for one. Does anyone remember Charlie Smith today, except as the answer to a trivia question? Funny game.

The problem with being a fringe player is that just about the time you get comfortable with a team, you're gone again. Wherever I had played, the scrubs banded together and developed our own esprit de corps. I don't think any of the teams ever suffered for it, although I am not sure all of my managers would agree. On the Phillies, we called ourselves The Avengers, and the group included Bobby Wine, Phil Linz and Jackie Brandt. Richie Allen was an honorary member. He was a great player, but he had the heart of a truant.

The career of another fellow, who was to become a special friend of mine, ended that year. Harvey Kuenn batted .296 for the Phillies and decided to call it a career. He was thirty-six, had played fifteen seasons and finished with a lifetime average of .303.

He had been a principal in one of the most publicized trades ever made. Harvey won the batting title at Detroit in 1959, and then was swapped for the man who had won the home run title, Rocky Colavito of Cleveland.

I admired Harvey as a fine agitator and one of the smartest hitters I had ever been around or caught behind. He stood in the deepest part of the batter's box and defied the pitcher to throw the ball on the outside corner of the plate. That was a pitch he could kill. He was an all-fields, line drive hitter, but if his team needed a run in the late innings to tie or win, he could take you downtown.

After our playing days, both of us came home to Milwaukee. Harvey joined the Brewers as a coach. I'm on the radio crew. And our friendship continues.

In February, three years ago, his right leg was

amputated because of a circulatory problem. By the end of spring training, he was walking on an artificial limb. By winter, he was playing golf every day. Sometimes a fellow as big and active as Harvey Kuenn finds it hard to accept such a blow. But those who knew him as a great athlete found out he was much more. He wouldn't let life slip one over the outside corner, either.

We were not far into the 1967 season when I knew my days with the Phillies were numbered. I went to the plate one night as a pinch hitter, and when I looked to the third-base coach for a sign he turned his back on me.

The trade that sent me back to the Braves, my original club, for another catcher, Gene Oliver, was announced on June seventh. In truth, I felt a little guilty about leaving Philadelphia. Richie Allen was brooding and threatening not to play. I felt like a hostage who had been released early.

The next morning, Rich said he wasn't going to the ball park anymore. I called Donald Davidson, the Braves' road secretary and an old friend, and told him I couldn't report right away. He pleaded with me: "Uke, dammit, you got to get your ass down here. Joe Torre is hurt and you're the only catcher we have."

When I left, Allen was still boycotting the ball park. Soon I heard from Charlie Meister, in the Phillies' front office: "You have to talk to Richie. He hasn't suited up since we made the trade." I called, reminded him that the Braves would be flying into Philadelphia for a three-game series that weekend, and convinced him to go back to work.

Of course, it didn't take much to keep Richie away from the ball park. He didn't like to practice. Always felt it wasn't in his contract. He had signed up just for the games.

I was fortunate to room with great, normal players like Eddie Mathews, and an occasional pure flake like Roger Craig.

Craig, my roomie in St. Louis, had one of the most uneven careers any pitcher ever had. He helped pitch the Dodgers to a pennant in 1959, and in two seasons with the Mets lost a total of forty-six games.

Influenced, perhaps, by his term with the Mets, Roger loved horror movies and sometimes imagined that he was in one. He had a problem with his neck for a while and wore a brace. I would open the closet door to put away my coat, and find him hanging on the inside of the door, his brace looped over the hook.

Those are the pictures you take out of baseball, more than the runs, hits, and errors. You remember the players and the people and the rhythm of the towns.

I honestly liked Philadelphia. The fans there were smart and mean and you could count on them. One of my biggest thrills in baseball was watching a guy fall out of the upper deck in Connie Mack Stadium. The crowd booed when he tried to get up.

On the other hand, I wasn't sure what to expect in Atlanta. The catching job would belong to Torre when he was well. But Paul Richards, the general manager, wanted to turn Phil Niekro into a starter, if he could find someone to catch his knuckleball.

The Braves had undergone many a change since I had last worn their uniform in 1963. For one thing, they were no longer in Milwaukee. Spahn, Burdette, Mathews and Crandall were gone.

When I walked into the Braves' clubhouse to rejoin the team I was given the white-carpet treatment. Literally. Joe Torre had laid out a path of white towels from the door to my new locker, above which were two handwritten signs. One, from Joe, had a heartfelt simplicity to it: THANK YOU VERY MUCH. GOD BLESS YOU.

The other said, LOTS OF LUCK. YOUR BUDDY, PHIL NIEKRO.

There was a third Brave eager to see me and renew an old acquaintance, Henry Aaron. Henry thought he had an old score to settle. The talk was just beginning to stir about his chances of breaking Ruth's career home-run record, and he accused me of taking one away from him in 1965.

Curt Simmons was on the mound that day for the Cardinals in St. Louis, Aaron had been frustrated by Simmons' assortment of slow curves. This time he ran up on the ball before the curve could break, and the pitch exploded off his bat, bouncing off the roof of the park in right field.

As Henry remembered it, I called the plate umpire's attention to the fact that he had stepped out of the batter's box. The umpire disallowed the homer and called him out.

The night I rejoined the Braves, Henry grinned and said, "If I miss Ruth's record by one homer, I'm going to be looking for you, Uecker."

I had to tell Henry the truth. It wasn't me. Tim McCarver was the catcher who took the homer away from him. But it was the sort of thing I would have been proud to do.

I was still a backup catcher, still the twenty-fourth or twenty-fifth man on the roster, still in the twilight of a mediocre career. But something was different this time. In a small way I had become necessary. All because of a maddening pitch that had carried Phil Niekro to the majors and now threatened to carry him right out.

It was a toss-up whether the batters hated to hit against Phil's knuckler as much as the catchers hated to catch it. He had played on teams in the minors where the catchers had simply refused. And he had lost more than one game when a third strike rolled back to the screen while the winning run crossed the plate.

I had caught Barney Schultz, in St. Louis, and Bob Tiefenauer, in Milwaukee, then the only other pitchers to rely almost exclusively on the knuckleball. I had one other thing going for me: my reputation as a defensive catcher. It occurred to me that when you don't hit much, teams tend to exaggerate your defensive skills.

I caught every game Niekro started the rest of the season, and I caught every day while Joe Torre recovered from his injury. In late June I had the biggest day at bat of my career, hitting my first grand-slam homer, off Ron Herbel of the Giants, and knocking in five runs.

Soon Niekro was giving me credit for keeping him in the big leagues. He was still doing it in 1981, fourteen years later. I don't know if this was the case, or a polite overstatement, but it was nice of Phil to say so. I am glad to claim him as the legacy of my big-league career. He won 150 games in those years, mostly for losing teams, and he is a fine legacy to have.

Niekro had a good slider and fastball, still has, but the knuckler was his strikeout pitch and he knew I wasn't afraid to call it with a runner at third. Every time he started I went through the same ritual before the game. I took four aspirin for the headache I knew I would have afterwards.

Once, after Phil had beaten the Pirates, 2-1, our trainer, Harvey Stone, looked up from rubbing his arm and told a reporter that Phil could probably pitch the next night.

Paul Richards overheard him. "No, he couldn't," Richards said, immediately.

"Why not?" asked the writer. "He needs more rest?"

"No," said Paul, "but Uecker does. Every time Niekro pitches, Uecker is the one who needs four days' rest."

Another problem with not having much talent is that it's hard to tell when you have begun to slip. But if I was on my way out of the big leagues, I was going more or less in style, and my fan club was going with me.

Baseball lore is filled with tearful stories of great players like Ruth and Mantle visiting hospitals and then slugging homers for a little sick kid. I made the same promise once, struck out three times and then found out the kid was an out-patient.

When it really counted, when it was not just a matter of drama but of justice, I am proud to say that I came through. When the Braves met the Cards in St. Louis on Sunday, July 23, Mark Stillwell showed up at Busch Stadium. Later, he described what happened: "There are in sports certain moments that come along perhaps only once in a lifetime. If you can take part in those special occurrences, you can treasure their memory always. If you miss them, you've missed them. The Home Run was such an occurrence.

"I was due to leave the twenty-fourth for Southern California to begin three years of active duty with the Navy. A Navy publication had recommended that the departing sailor should endeavor to spend his last hours at home with his loved ones. I did just that. I drove to St. Louis to see the Cardinals play a doubleheader with the Braves . . ."

I sat out the opener as the Braves lost, 3-1. In the nightcap, I started and struck out my first time out. Mark continues: "When he came up in the fourth with one out and nobody on, I snapped a picture of him taking a cut at the plate. A couple of pitches later Uecker got around on what was probably a hanging curve and hit a long fly ball down the line toward left field. It looked like just a routine fly ball and it hadn't sounded particularly solid but it kept carrying, and carrying, and finally fell deep into the loge reserved seats in left field for Uecker's third homer of the year.

"As Uecker started the home-run trot around the base paths, I realized what I had just witnessed. I set up a clamor like few around me could believe or understand. It dawned on me that I was the only guy yelling for Uecker in the entire crowd . . . I may well have been the only member of the Uecker Fan Club ever to see The Great One crack a home run."

In retrospect we know how he must have felt. I am told that some people never forget the first time they heard Heifitz play the violin, or Caruso sing an aria, or watched the sun set on Bo Derek's body. The homer had no bearing on the outcome of the game, which the Cards won, 8-3, to sweep the doubleheader. Of the thousands who were there, only two of us had any reason to care or remember it, and I am not so sure about myself.

So much for history. The Braves finished sixth and fired manager Billy Hitchcock. I played in eighty games, the most of my career, and hit .150, my lowest ever. I did lead the league in one category, and I could not have done it without Phil Niekro. I was charged with twenty-seven passed balls. The next-highest total was sixteen.

I kept intact my career record of never having stolen a base or legged out a triple. It was a letdown to the kids at Drury College, but I hoped they would overcome it in time.

And so the stage was set for the series of events I have described earlier: the accident on Clete Boyer's motorcycle, the barroom fight in Fort Lauderdale, my release as a player and coach, then signing with the Braves as a speaker and occasional broadcaster.

In 1971, Alan (Bud) Selig offered me a chance to return to Milwaukee as a full-time member of the radio crew. I jumped at it, completing a cycle as the first Milwaukee boy signed by the Braves, traded by the Braves, fired by the Braves, and hired by the Brewers.

As I think back on the zaniness of my years, I am grateful for the career I had. I mean, one good season and I might have blown my entire future in broadcasting. Today I speak frequently at banquets around the country, and the audiences often include youngsters. I always try to leave them with one sincere thought. If you can't play a sport . . . the hell with it.

As for the fan club, I never really felt that I deserved it. Of course, I have arthritis in one knee and I don't feel I deserve that, either.

And I am still in touch with Mark Stillwell, who was born to be a public relations man, and whose enthusiasm now serves the football Cardinals. After I had begun to appear as a repeat guest on the *Tonight Show*, I received a long and nostalgic letter from Mark. He closed by saying: "My brother asked me last week what the greatest satisfaction from the fan club had been. I told him it was being able to say that we had followed your career from the time you were a tuba player for the 1964 World Champions."

PART III

Outside Baseball

*In which he looks at the world of radio and
television; and a strike that could have
hurt everyone except Bob Uecker, who can
always go back into the service.*

"He (Dave Winfield) also wanted a voice in team
trades, more beef in the ground patties, and the right
to change his name to Ronald McWinfield."

7. All My Tonights

WHEN ANYONE ASKS ME how to break into radio and television, I never know where to begin. Or where to end. I might tell them this truth: You have to be lucky. It isn't enough just to be crazy.

The only training I ever had was as an occasional guest on a postgame show. Of course, I also called the play-by-play of hundreds of games for the boys in the bullpen, broadcasting into a beer cup.

My career is a confirmation of one of the basic laws of success: Anything is obtainable if you don't need it.

There are advantages to not being a star athlete. When you retire no one feels cheated, and the adjustment to the Real World is more gentle, emotionally as well as financially. Some athletes need a decompression chamber when the time comes to take off the uniform. They suffer withdrawal pains when the cheering stops.

While it lasted, while the player was hot, the wine flowed and the dollies came waltzing through the green pastures and big offers and big deals became a part of his daily routine. Later the offers turned small and the deals disappeared.

The fringe player doesn't miss the cheers and his standard of living doesn't undergo a dramatic change. My highest salary in baseball was twenty-three thousand dollars. In a few years I would be earning more than that, from telling people what a failure I was.

I was perfectly content with my life in Atlanta in 1969, working in the speaker's bureau for the Braves and doing the color on their telecasts. Now and then I did a turn at the Playboy Club, managed by a friend of mine, John Barnes, who had once run the business end of Al Hirt's club in New Orleans.

That year Barnes talked Al into opening a saloon next to the Playboy Club, featuring the Dixieland sound and look, with jazz and red wall fabric.

Hirt flew in for the opening of the club and John asked me to ride out to the airport with him to meet the great trumpet player. Al got off the plane wearing a Cossack hat and a full-length fur coat and a dark beard. You got this overpowering impression of *fur*. If he had landed in the Himalayas, the natives would have set traps for him.

It was because of Al Hirt that I became a frequent guest on the *Tonight Show*, a debt I will describe later.

Even before we shook hands I knew we would hit it off. I began to rip him immediately about his size. Al is the best kind of friend to have, the kind you can't embarrass, and vice versa. And we have both tried.

Every November I try to spend three weeks in New Orleans, working with Al in his club on Bourbon Street. It has become a tradition. We drink, we jam, we fish. I have never found a more fulfilling way to spend my time. The part I enjoy most is not drowning.

Once, after an all-night jam session at the club, we

·drove to Shell Beach, Louisiana, a forty-minute drive from New Orleans, to the fishing camp where Al keeps a boat. He filled a cooler with sandwiches and beer and booze. The party included his clarinetist, Pee Wee, and his brother, Little Gerald, who is the same size as Al and looks just like him except that his beard is red.

Al and I climbed into one boat, a twenty-eight-foot whaler, and the others, Pee Wee, Gerald and a couple of fellows from the club, climbed into a larger one. We were still feeling frisky from the night before when we headed for the bayous, fifteen or twenty miles out. It was a damp, chilly morning and Al had on his Russian outfit, the hat and coat, with the collar turned up. The other boat took the lead and we followed, with Al at the controls.

We were going wide open through the canals, curving and hooking, kicking up a spray on either side of us. I was sitting forward in the whaler and saw the first boat make a wide turn. We didn't seem to be slowing and I suddenly realized Al was going to have to cut it pretty short if we were going to make the turn. So I looked over my shoulder to say something and I discovered that Al was fast asleep.

When I realized there was no hope of making the turn I began to scream at Al, my face reddening in the wind. The swamps were coming up fast. When I saw he wasn't going to wake up, much less throttle back, I stood up in the front of the boat. I am not sure why I did, unless it was to get a closer look at the disaster rushing to meet us. When we hit the bog I was like a missile going through the saw grass.

I landed face down, arms out, covered with muck and mud, and with only two thoughts on my mind: ALLIGATORS AND SNAKES.

I struggled to my feet, rising out of the primeval goop, which was like quicksand, and turned to walk back to the boat. What I saw looked like a scene from *Boom Town*, with mud flying thirty feet in the air, as though we had brought in oil. The engines were still wide open. When I pulled myself back aboard, Al was no longer sitting in the same spot. He was on his hands and knees with his head stuck in the bait box. I yanked him up by the back of his coat. He was still asleep, live shrimp dangling from his beard like weird Christmas ornaments.

The group on the other boat had watched with horror as we went aground. They came alongside, their faces pale and anxious. That was their meal ticket sitting there, slumped over the bait box. Gerald said, "Christ, what happened?"

"Al was showing me a scene from 'Victory at Sea'," I said. "The son of a bitch fell asleep, going thirty miles an hour. We were wide open."

Finally, Al yawned and opened his eyes. When it became obvious he was unhurt, we all started laughing so hard nobody could speak. He looked at us suspiciously as he picked the shrimp out of his beard.

Another time I went out with Al and Pee Wee. On the way in, Al decided to sleep and he stretched out on the floor between a fishing chair and the side of the boat. We docked, took off the fishing gear and unloaded, then woke him up. He didn't move. "Hey, I'm stuck," he yelled. "I can't get out."

We thought he was joking. But he was wedged in. I don't know if the boat shrank or Al expanded, but it took us fifteen minutes of maneuvering to get him out of there. The longer it took the more nervous and ill-tempered he got. He had visions of becoming a permanent fixture, like the figurehead on a Viking sailing vessel. I had a great plan for getting him out of there quickly, but we couldn't find a harpoon.

Al Hirt has a heart bigger than a bass fiddle. When I married my wife, Judy, he made all the arrangements, picking the day, the church, the minister, and the music. He likes people, enjoys their successes, and is just as comfortable in the company of a Catholic priest as he is in that of a baseball player.

One of his closest friends in New Orleans was the fire and police chaplain, Father Pete Rogers. He would tell people, proudly: "Fodda Pete leads the world in talking guys down offa bridges. How many you talked down this year, Fodda? Seventeen?" Al would shake his head. "He's a great man. If I was the boss I'd make him pope."

Al was a child prodigy who could play the trumpet at six. At Jesuit High, in New Orleans, he was on the football team as a sophomore, changing uniforms at the half so he could march with the band. His father, a cop, made him quit football to concentrate on his music.

He owned a small piece of the New Orleans Saints in the early years. At the games he would walk through the stands and swing into "When the Saints Go Marching In." The noise of the crowd would explode, until opposing teams complained they could not hear the signals. Now Al only plays for the Super Bowl and other religious holidays.

And while it is true that in professional sports many owners can sing the blues, Al Hirt is the only one I know who ever made a living at it.

I knew the first time we met that he was my kind of degenerate. When Al opened the club in Atlanta, he invited me to take the stage during his breaks. I did a half hour of what I usually do. After the show, Al's agent,

Jerry Purcell, approached me. He asked me if I'd like to appear on the *Tonight Show.*

I thought to myself, "Yeah, sure, the *Tonight Show.* Me and ten million other characters."

Ten days later, I found myself walking through a curtain and taking a seat on a couch next to Johnny Carson. Purcell had called and told me to fly to New York. I went on that night, after meeting with Carson's talent coordinator, Craig Tennis.

That night, for one of the few times in my life, I was scared spitless. I was not a comic. Never thought of myself as one. I had performed in nightclubs and not been nervous, partly because I was always half boiled. I walked around backstage, trying to keep straight in my mind what I wanted to say. No one knew who the hell I was. I don't remember seeing any other faces. There were people there, but they didn't seem to have faces. That was how I knew I was nervous.

Whatever I said that night worked. The audience laughed. After the show I heard Carson turn to Ed McMahon and ask, "Is this guy really a baseball player?"

Three weeks after the first time, I was invited back. What happened next was not exactly the classic show biz story, with instant stardom and headlines in *Variety.* Nor did I rush out and hire an agent named Max.

But my career began to move. My speaking fees rose. ABC hired me to be a part of the original crew for *Monday Night Baseball.* I was signed to be a guest host on other national shows, such as *The Midnight Special.* For a guy who spent the better part of his life behind a mask, I suddenly had a face people knew.

Whatever the benefits of being on the *Tonight Show,* I accepted them without guilt or pressure. I have been a guest always for the fun of it—mine, if not theirs. I don't consider what I do to be show business. Or journalism. Or an art form. Or even a business. I don't consider it to be a lot of things. I broadcast sports, mostly baseball. My work is to these other things what recess is to school.

But I saw quickly that the exposure on the *Tonight Show* was terrific, the best stage ever created for anyone with a movie, TV series, song, or toy to sell. Of course, what makes it all work is Johnny Carson, his wit, discipline, and generosity.

If I were to rate Carson in baseball terms, I would say he can do it all: hit, hit with power, field, and throw. I don't know if he can run. It is hard to tell about a man you usually see sitting behind a desk.

I am not sure that even his most devoted fans really understand what Carson has achieved. There is simply no one else in the field to compare with him, with the freshness and endurance of the show he has done night after night, year after year. Though himself a master comic, he is probably the finest straight man alive. I found him generous when it counts most, when no one is watching. During a station break, sitting there, chatting idly, he would coach me a little: "You ought to be saying more about this," or "drop in another line about that."

As many amateurs do, I had a habit of protecting myself by warning him: "You've probably heard this one . . ." Johnny assured me, "Hey, I don't hear every joke in the world."

There is a kind of art to the way he puts you at ease, once you slip into the chair next to his. You can sense the empathy he has for a struggling comic or singer. He is a contained and private man, even with his staff, but not in a selfish way. I admire him for trying to keep his personal life separate from the show and his career.

I have a theory about Carson. I believe one reason he has survived so long, and so well, is that he has less ego than his critics think. He isn't always drawn to the center of the stage. He doesn't have to be "on" all the time.

Some performers feel obligated to crack jokes to a bunch of strangers riding in an elevator. I understand that feeling. Part of my disposition demands that people find me funny or amusing. If I were on a show, or at a banquet, and the laughs didn't come, I would drop my pants. Anything. I would get that laugh.

Carson would merely shrug, do a Jack Benny pause, and go on to the next one.

I never had the same determination about baseball, and maybe that was my undoing. No matter how badly I wanted to get a base hit, I knew the other guy was trying to stop me. And I might be overmatched. In front of an audience, no one can stop me but myself. The audience is on your side (usually).

I feel fortunate to have been on the *Tonight Show* when there occurred one or more Unforgettable Moments. I was a guest the night Burt Reynolds sat in for Johnny, and another guest was his ex-wife, Judy Carne, the actress and comedienne, who had emerged as a star of the new hit show, *Laugh-In*.

Burt took me aside backstage and confided, a bit nervously, that they had not seen each other since their divorce, three years or so earlier. "I don't know what the hell is going to happen," he said, "so if it gets a little tense or shaky feel free to jump in."

I came out first, then Judy, then Helen Gurley Brown, the editor of *Cosmopolitan*. It was the night Helen suggested that Burt pose for the centerfold in *Cosmo*. We all played around with that thought for a while, and Burt asked if I would do such a thing. I said, "Sure. As long as they'd let me wear a pair of shin-guards, I'd be all right."

Judy teasingly suggested that he could cover himself with his hand, and Burt immediately shouted, "You mean MY ARM, MY ARM."

The show was bright and funny. My own impression was that there still existed a warm affection between Burt and Judy. And, of course, he did pose for *Cosmopolitan*.

I was on another night with a guest named Foster Brooks, listed on the schedule as a professor from Harvard, or some such. We chatted backstage. I did my bit, and then Foster was introduced, and the moment he walked through the curtain I thought, "Oh, jeezus, the guy is plastered. Fifteen minutes ago he was sober, now he's just destroyed." I was embarrassed for him, until I realized, about the time the audience did, that he was doing his drunk act. He was hilarious. And later I learned he doesn't drink at all.

Don Rickles used to tape his television series, *CPO Sharkey*, in the studio next to the *Tonight Show*, and I would drop by to watch him work. I discovered early that I could play on his insecurity. It's true; like most comics, Don is sensitive and his feelings are easily bruised.

We developed a kind of ritual. He always asked me how I liked his show.

"Okay," I would say, forcing the word. "It was okay."

"No, dammit, how did you like it?"

"It was okay," I repeated, "but it wasn't you."

Now Rickles would give me that ear-to-ear grin, the one that makes him look like he should be sitting on a lily pad. "No, really, what did you think?"

"Hey, Don, if you want me to say it was great, if that's what you need to hear, yeah, it was great."

Then I would walk away and, over my shoulder, I'd whisper, "But it's not you."

Rickles is a fanatic about baseball and most other sports. He wasn't big enough to play sports in school, he says, "But I was always the kid who helped the gym teacher take the names of those who weren't practicing."

He can create a caricature, even his own, with words. "Actually," he says, "I would like to be a general manager and have the guys come and get them girls and sit and drink with them and tell them what bad years they had."

Once I offered to leave tickets for him any time the Brewers were in town to play the California Angels. His eyes lighted up. He said, "My kid really loves baseball. Do you think you could take him down to the clubhouse and show him around?"

I promised I would. Rickles was in Las Vegas when the next trip rolled around, but I called his house and talked to his son, a pre-teenager.

"This is Bob Uecker," I said.

"So what?" he said.

"I promised your dad I'd leave you tickets to the ballgame."

"Who cares?" he said.

The kid didn't go to the game. To this day I think Rickles put him up to it. Or else he is a Dodger fan.

The real pleasure, for me, of being on the *Tonight Show* was the chance it provided to meet and work with Burt Reynolds and Rickles, and other guest hosts such as David Brenner, David Letterman, Bob Newhart, Robert Klein, David Hartman and Joey Bishop—all these in addition to Johnny.

Not even Avis has gotten more mileage out of being Number 2 than Ed McMahon. The friendship of Ed and John, their loyalty, the fun they have, is part of what makes the *Tonight Show* an appealing place to be. Another key is the quality of the staff, starting with Freddie de Cordova, the producer; Jack Grant, the stage manager; Craig Tennis, Ginny Fosdick, Shirley Woods, and the fellows in the booth, Bob Ostberg and Bobby Quinn.

Many a night I have sat backstage for hours after a show with Tommy Newsom or Doc Severinsen, and the guys in the band, having a few pops and talking baseball.

There is no need to pinpoint which night it was that almost didn't end, causing me to nearly miss a baseball broadcast for the only time in my career. Nor will I mention which member of the staff was with me when I so nearly disgraced myself.

I didn't think I had a problem when I missed my flight at 10:00 P.M. I could still catch a breakfast flight in time to join the Brewers in New York for the game the next evening against the Yankees. And I would not have had a problem, except for a slight miscalculation. My plane was not leaving from the airport where my friend dropped me that morning, in a condition less than clear-headed.

The clerks at the airline counter were bemused, and offered me a place to lie down, when I tried to explain that the Brewers were in New York, I was in the wrong airport, and my partner, Merle Harmon, was off somewhere televising a World Football League game. There was no one else to do the radio broadcast.

While my ticket was being changed, I placed a frantic phone call to Bob Sullivan, the team's equipment man, at the hotel in New York. I tried to sound calm, but after about thirty seconds of his saying, "I can't understand you, what was that?" I realized it wasn't working.

Finally, I said, "Look, Sully, get hold of Tom Ferguson and go up to the booth when the game starts." (Ferguson, now a vice-president and traveling secretary with the Brewers, had started out as a clubhouse boy with the Braves.) "Just open the show for me. Talk about anything. Talk about the difference in laundry prices in New York and what it costs to clean the uniforms. I'll get there as early as I can."

It looked as though baseball was about to record another first. An equipment man was going to open the radio broadcast of a game between the Yankees and the Brewers. Alas, I got the next flight out, grabbed a cab to the ball park, and collapsed in the booth five minutes before air time.

I don't think Sully or Fergie will ever forgive me for depriving them of his big chance.

8. The Boys in the Booth

MY TRAVELS LED ME one summer to what I thought would be a quiet night in Cincinnati, the kind of night you expect in Cincinnati. I should have known better.

It was the Sunday before a Monday night baseball game, to be televised over ABC. Sharing my table in the hotel dining room were Howard Cosell and Chet Forte, our director.

Cosell and Forte have known each other for years, ever since Chet was the nation's leading scorer in basketball his senior year at Columbia. Once, before a game, Chet agreed to be a guest on Howard's radio show. As they waited for a cue, the little guard asked, "What are we going to talk about, Howard?"

"Relax, kid," said Cosell. "Leave it to me. You'll do fine."

Whereupon Howard opened the interview, turned to his guest and said, "Chet, is it true that some of your teammates hate to pass to you because you shoot so much?"

As Rick said to Louie on the airstrip at Casablanca, it was the start of a great relationship. Chet knows Cosell so well that he is able to finish most of his meals, no matter how much Howard agitates the people around him. And Howard is one of the most artful agitators of this or any other time.

In the middle of dinner, two young ladies approached our table to confirm that the voice they were hearing really belonged to Howard Cosell. On a good night, Howard's voice can be heard in every corner of a restaurant, into the kitchen, and out the service door.

An incurable flirt, although a harmless one, Howard soon had a dialogue going with the one named Cindy, a blonde in her early twenties. When he learned that their boyfriends were at a table a few feet away, he raised his voice and said, "If those fellows continue to bother you, my dear, I am going to send Bob Uecker over there to break their legs."

Every few minutes, Howard would toss off a line of that general substance, and I began to get some hard looks from their table. I made a mental note of the fact that both were young and burly and they were drinking, not eating. Cindy was enjoying Cosell's attention, and I guessed that it was only a matter of time until her friend came over and hauled her away. You get a premonition about those things and you can almost put a watch to it.

Soon enough, this brute of a guy sidled up to the table and stood there looking puzzled. He put a hand lightly on the girl's shoulder, but before he could speak Howard warned him, "If you touch Cindy again I'll have Uecker tear your head off."

At that point, I leaned across the table, my chin almost touching the butter dish, and whispered: "Howie, I just want you to know something. This guy may drop me, but if I have time to get off one punch, you're going down with me."

As luck would have it, he was as curious about Cosell as she was. There was no menace in him, although you would not have been reassured if all you had heard was his name and avocation. His name was Tyrone Malone and he drag-raced SEMIS. He invited us out to the hotel parking lot in the morning for a demonstration.

When we arrived at the parking lot after breakfast, we rubbed our eyes in disbelief. He had three huge trailers painted red, white, and blue, with enough chrome on them to make the Hell's Angels weep. Probably cost a half million each. A tractor was attached to the back of one. Behind another was a truck, on the back of which was a frozen whale, with a catwalk leading up to it so people could get a close look.

In the mouth of the whale was a photograph, an eight-by-ten glossy of Gregory Peck, taken from a scene in the movie *Moby Dick*.

I have no idea how long that whale had been on the back of that truck. I did not ask. All I know is, that odor was the foulest I have ever smelled in my life, and I am a guy who has been in a baseball locker room after a doubleheader when the second game went eighteen innings.

Naturally, Tyrone Malone wanted to know if one of us would like to join him for a run in the parking lot, to get a feeling for this kind of drag racing. Naturally, Howard and Chet insisted they could not deny me this honor.

I took a pack of cigarettes and tucked them in my shirt sleeve and rolled up the sleeve the way I had seen drag racers do in the movies. Then I climbed into the cab of that monster next to Tyrone Malone, who is a six-footer, about 230, with brown hair and arms larger than most people's legs. He was leaning out the window, watching Cindy kick out the tire blocks, and telling me out the side of his mouth how he travels to fairs all over the country, drag racing his semis. I noticed Cosell and Forte moving back, smiling and flashing me the victory sign.

Tyrone dropped it in gear—he put it on the floor, as they say in CB talk—and announced: "I'm going to put the hammer down now."

I said, "Do whatever you want. I'm just along for the ride."

Tires smoking, he proceeded to run that baby through the parking lot, one hundred fifty yards long, and had the truck up to sixty miles an hour when he hit the brake. I was amazed that a diesel that size could burn rubber. After that run, he backed up and made another. I rattled around in that cab like a dice in a cup, the truck was vibrating so hard.

When I stumbled out of the cab, Chet and Howard said they were trying to remember the last time they laughed so hard. They thought and thought, but didn't come up with anything.

The first six years of my career with ABC—I started in 1975—went pretty much in this vein, by accident or design I can't say. In a sense I am their off-the-wall editor, the Walter Mitty of the staff, the fellow who will try anything once, or even twice, if once is not enough.

The baseball strike of 1981 afforded me a rare chance to report on the world lumberjack championships at Hayward, Wisconsin, held every July, in what would normally be the heart of the hardball season.

Lumberjacking is a hugely popular sport in Australia and New Zealand, and in our upper central and northwestern states, where the timber industry is strong. They have a circuit, a mystique, and a following all their own, like rodeo.

On the first day of competition one fellow fell seventy feet and broke both his legs. In the speed climb, their tools are a telephone lineman's spike and a safety rope. They pull themselves to the top of a one-hundred-foot pole cut from a California redwood—the amateurs stop at seventy feet—ring a bell and then descend. Some go down so quickly they scrape the skin off their arms. The man who fell lost his safety strap.

These are among the strongest, bravest, craziest characters in the world. I watched them and wondered how our best athletes would compete against them. That is, if they could get in the same kind of shape, able to saw through a thirty-inch log in twenty-four seconds, using a chain saw powered by a motorcycle engine.

In another event, they put a thirty-inch log between their legs, raise an axe sharpened like a straight razor, and at the gun split the log with three or four swings. One guy had the wrong angle on one swing and almost took off his right calf.

On the third day, there was a break from the log rolling and axe swinging and pole climbing, and the TV crew and the contestants relaxed on a moonlight sail along the Namagagon (an old Indian word meaning fielder's choice). I joined the jacks for drinks and good talk.

You would not mistake any of them for adagio dancers. They were huge men, most with beards, their humor robust and earthy. I found that they needled and insulted each other just as baseball players do, and I jumped right in.

As the boat glided along, and the drinks went down smooth, I asked a New Zealander named Jim Wass if what I had heard was true: that a lumberjack was so tough he could shave himself with an axe.

He said, yeah, it was true.

I told him Americans were tough, too, and I vaguely remember making a speech about Paul Bunyan and his blue ox Babe. At one point I asked Wass if he thought he could shave me, if I was having an appendectomy. I am not sure what the appendectomy had to do with anything, or where I had in mind his shaving me, but he said, yeah, he could.

The next day I had forgotten the whole conversation. We had set up our cameras in front of the grandstand, which encircled a small lake. There was a pier nearby where the lumberjacks did their chopping. We had a clear view of the pit on the other side, where two hundred-foot pole rose against the sky, and two men climbed at a time.

Our producer, Ellie Riger, came up to me and asked if I was ready to go. I thought she was talking about an interview, and I looked around me, sort of absently, and asked, "Anyone special you want me to talk to?"

She said, "No, I want you to do the shaving thing."

I said, "The shaving thing?"

She nodded.

Just then Jim Wass strolled up, cradling a five-pound, single-bladed axe. The conversation of the night before started to come back to me. I heard myself say, "Oh, God, I was only kidding about the appendicitis."

But I was game. And I knew instinctively that the film would be something nice to stick in the show, the tough-but-oh-so-gentle shtick. People were moving around and rearranging cameras. Wass took out a pumice stone and started sharpening his axe.

I watched closely for a moment, then asked, "Is this thing going to do the job?"

He spit on his arm, wet it down and shaved a patch of hair. Then he looked up at me and said, "Don't worry about it."

I still did not feel quite the level of confidence I felt the stunt demanded. Every few minutes Wass would test the blade. The third time he cut himself and a small ribbon of blood ran across his arm.

I thought to myself, maybe this guy isn't as good as he says he is, or else we should have gone home earlier last night. Out loud I said, "Look, try that on my arm." So I wet my arm and the hair wouldn't come off. The blade would not shave my arm. I wondered about my face. I don't consider myself vain, but whether you are handsome or ugly, it is nice to have a face.

It was too late to back out. I touched the blade with my finger and it really did feel sharp as a razor. So I sat on a log, and while the cameras rolled and a few people shot still pictures, Jim got out a can of cream and I lathered up. He proceeded to shave me just like a barber, lifting my nose, tightening the skin under my neck.

As soon as he started I could tell he knew what he was doing. I looked down at the ground where the wood chips were and I didn't see any blood, and I didn't hear anybody cry out, "Oh, shit!" So I knew it was okay.

If I have a weakness, or even a talent, for ideas that are slightly off center, it wasn't something I developed for network television. It is an extension of what I have been doing all my life.

A few years ago, as a promotion, the Brewers decided to inflate a hot-air balloon before a game at County Stadium. Merle Harmon suggested that we could make history by doing a part of the broadcast from inside the gondola of the balloon. Specifically, my part of the broadcast.

The balloon, they assured me, would be tethered to a light tower and would not be allowed to rise above a couple hundred feet. We would not ascent at all if the winds were over twelve hundred feet because the stadium was in the landing pattern for the airport in Milwaukee, Mitchell Field.

On Saturday morning, the day of the game, the first thing I did was check the weather. It was windy as hell outside. I felt a surge of relief as I left for the park.

People were clutching their hats and women's skirts were flapping as I walked through the press gate. Hot-dog wrappers and small objects whipped through the stands. The players were bending against the wind as I walked onto the field.

And in front of the fence in center field, the ground crew was trying to blow up the balloon. They had decided to at least do the pregame show from the gondola. The pilot, or captain, was directing the work, which had a certain mad urgency about it. The gondola was on its side, and things began to go badly as soon as they turned on the gas. The guy who was fluffing up the silk was burned by the flamethrower they use to heat the air, and needed first aid.

The captain told me, over the howl of the wind, that we would get her airborne, have the ground crewmen hold the lines, and let the balloon float around the park for a while. The crowd would love it, he assured me.

I climbed into the gondola with the unhappiest-looking radio engineer in captivity. We went on the air, and I tried to do the pregame show, and the wind kept tipping over the gondola. We were bouncing up and down like a golf ball on a driveway, and the guys on the ground crew were running around in all directions, eight or ten of them, trying to hang on to the ropes.

We would get up about fifteen feet, then bang down and tip over. I was hanging on to a safety bar with one hand, holding on to the microphone with the other, and my feet kept flying out from under me. The captain was yelling up at us, telling me to stop kicking the gas tanks, I was letting out the air.

We must have looked like those early slow-motion films of the rockets that kept falling off the launching pad. After twenty minutes of banging up and down, the gondola turned over and dumped us out, like kittens from a basket. The crowd never did figure out what we were supposed to be doing, but they loved every turbulent minute of it. When the engineer and I crawled off the field, they cheered.

As far as I know, that was the last time anyone attempted to broadcast a baseball game from a hot-air balloon.

Given the record of my own playing days, the bosses at ABC clearly decided that I was qualified to work on a show called *The Superstars*. I have done several, and my speciality has become the unusual, if not impossible, scene-set.

The first *Superstars* show I ever helped report, in 1976, I made my arrival by sea. Bob Goodrich and Roger Goodman, the director and producer of the show, had brought the crew to the Bahamas, where the water sparkles in the noonday sun and the sands are as fine as salt. They asked if I could suggest something funny for the opener. I said the first thing that popped into my head: "Why don't I put on a suit of clothes and swim in?"

Their eyes got big as saucers. Bob said, "Would you really do it?"

When I saw them next they were toting a box from a discount store in Freeport. It contained a double-breasted coat, slacks, shirt, and tie. Fully dressed, I waded about one hundred yards out into the water.

On the beach, Al Michaels, Don Drysdale and Reggie Jackson opened the show. Al mentioned the fact that Bob Uecker was supposed to be there but had not yet arrived. In the background, you could see me behind them, fighting my way through the surf.

I finally made it ashore and dragged myself onto the catamaran. The three of them all shouted, "Uke's here," and Drysdale looked me over and asked what happened.

Panting, I replied, "I had some extra time, so instead of flying to Freeport I took a boat. We were having a party and it got kind of loud and the captain told us to quiet down. We ignored him and started throwing bottles over the rail with notes. He came back a second time and told us either to get quiet or he'd put me overboard. I told him he didn't have the guts, and that was the last thing I remember."

We were back in Freeport in 1976, after the Olympics in Montreal. This time we did a scene-set—in the middle of the summer—with me decked out in a full winter ski outfit, trying to ski down the sand to Frank Gifford, Don Meredith and Reggie Jackson. I had supposedly taken a wrong turn on the cross-country trail in Montreal, and ended up on the beach at Freeport.

The joke worked fine, except for the fact that I had never skied before, the boots were a size eight and a half and I wear a ten, and we had to do three or four takes while the sweat poured out of me as though from a

THE MAN
WHO MADE
MEDIOCRITY
FAMOUS.

Left, looking for my contact lens.

Below, umpire and batter (Doug Rader) pay no attention as I faint after finally catching this knuckleball.

The young player is easy prey for seductive baseball groupies such as Phyllis Diller.

D. ELLIOTT

Big league athletes are subjected to the most malicious and unfounded rumors (Number 6 is Clete Boyer).

Left, Dick Bertell (Cubs) slides in. The worst part of being a catcher is always having your back to the camera.

Right, Tony Cloninger (Braves) slides in.

Above, Rico Carty (Braves) slides in.

Below, Harvey Kuenn (Giants) slides in.

T. MCDONOUGH

Above, John Roseboro (Dodgers) slides in.
Below, Vada Pinson (Reds) slides in.

Above, Cardinals call time to review my performance.

Below, Being forcibly removed from the game
(by my own team).

Here I am trying to score from second on a three-base hit; out on a close play.

Celebration in Cardinal clubhouse after team announced I would not play in 1967 World Series; Carl Warwick pours.

BOB
UECKER
MILWAUKEE BRAVES   C

One of my first bubble gum cards.

I tricked the Topps people by posing lefthanded; no one noticed.

CARDS

CATCHER
BOB UECKER

With Del Crandall and Joe Torre in Milwaukee; too bad the other two never made it.

Once again the guys told me it was a night game; with Del Crandall, Henry Aaron, and Ed Mathews.

Joe Garagiola made the airwaves safe for ex-catchers.

Original Monday Night Baseball crew—Warner Wolf,
Bob Prince and Bob Uecker became household words
(the household was in Menomonee Falls, Wisconsin).

The cleanest shave I ever had; at World Lumberjack Championships.

Yes, Johnny, I am...

Al Hirt and me filming a segment for the
Un-American Sportsman.

Al Hirt points me to the stage, I think.

A man for all seasons.

Diving for scuba in the Bahamas.

Portrait of a star.

garden hose. Of course, I didn't really ski. I just sort of shuffled along, with a pole in each hand, yodeling as I went.

Another time I was to do an opening with Gifford at the swimming pool, and Frank wasn't told what to expect. I put on every piece of equipment I could find that would be used in the *Superstars*: flippers, a snorkel mask, a pair of size nineteen tennis shoes over my neck, a bowling ball in one hand and a tennis racket under my arm. I came walking out and Frank looked up from his commentary just in time to see me talking through the snorkel. He got on a laughing jag and it took us six takes to get through the scene.

They are a good gang to work with, Keith Jackson, Michaels, Gifford, the entire SS army. I have a special respect for Chet Forte, a small, dark, snappy fellow who has won seven or eight Emmy awards. More important, his sense of humor is as warped as mine.

It was Forte who came up with the idea for the Gorilla Trick.

For years, on the football side of Monday night, Cosell had conducted a running gag with me as the target. Whenever a team appeared with a mascot, or a fan dressed in a chicken suit, or as an owl or a robot or a horse, anything weird, Howard would say, "Well . . . I . . . see . . . Bob Uecker . . . is . . . here . . . tonight."

Then Gifford and Meredith and Fran Tarkenton picked it up and began to act as Howard's spotter: "Hey, Howard, there's Uecker," pointing to someone dressed as a bumblebee or a duck.

In December of 1980, Chet called me from Miami, where he was to direct a game between the Dolphins and

New England. I was to fly down a few days later to film another *Superstars* show. He asked if I could fly in early, and be there in time for the game.

A car was waiting for me at the airport Monday afternoon. I was taken by the freight elevator to my room in the Sonesta Beach Hotel, and stayed there until the broadcasting crew—Cosell, Gifford and Tarkenton—left for the Orange Bowl.

At the stadium I went directly to the truck and waited there with Forte and Bob Goodrich. We watched the game on the monitor. At one point, Chet punched up a picture of a guy in a Santa Claus suit. Gifford said, "There's Bob Uecker."

Cosell added, "Yes, he's just back from the baseball winter meetings."

A canary feather all but fluttered from Chet Forte's smiling lips. "Now's the time," he said. I felt like an agent about to be dropped behind enemy lines. They had gone to a costume store and purchased a gorilla outfit. I slipped into the suit, walked into the end zone and put on the mask. A technician with a hand-held camera was ready to cue me as soon as the boys mentioned my name.

He gave me the cue.

I took off the gorilla mask.

A sort of gargling noise came from Cosell's throat. It was beautiful.

If Howard Cosell personally found the answer to poverty, high interest rates, and bad officiating, there would be those who criticized him. The truth is, Howard is the kind of guy who will pull you out of a ditch. He performs countless acts of kindness, large and small, without getting (or wanting) credit for them.

On the Sunday before the baseball strike, Cosell flew

into Kansas City for the telecast on Monday night of the game between the Royals and the Yankees. That afternoon the Brewers were in town.

Howard caught a cab from the airport to the park, sat in the booth the entire game and kept up a running repartee with my partners and me. I compared him to Richard Arlen, the old, stylish actor who always wore a scarf.

Howard repaid the compliment by saying, "Personally, Uke, I don't understand what Bud Selig sees in you or why he keeps you on the air."

At the end of the game, as he left the booth, I said, "Nice to have seen you, Howie."

He said, "I wish I could say the same."

When Cosell was unable to appear at a roast and toast in my honor in Milwaukee, he sent instead a tape-recorded message. Imagine you can hear Howard's voice—it should not be difficult—as you read these words.

"People who have studied baseball in Milwaukee from its very beginning usually associate the sport with such names as Aaron and Mathews, Spahn and Burdette and Logan and Adcock and Bruton, and all the rest from the halcyon days of the Braves.

"And now those who are contemporary think of Caldwell and Hisle and that brilliant band of youngsters who are on the field for a young and promising and exciting team. You can throw in Bando's name, if you will, though he is hardly worthy of mention [note: Sal Bando was at the banquet] . . . but the point is, those of us on the inside of the so-called national pastime *know* that only two names ever really mattered in Milwaukee baseball . . . Osinski and Uecker. Osinski, of the spitball, and Uecker, of the knuckle head. Matter of fact, Bob, the more I've watched your career in broadcasting, the more it has made me realize the truth of what I have so often said, that there are only two professions in America where you can begin at the top. Prostitution and sportscasting.

"I don't know what your plans are for the rest of your life, but one thing is certain. You have got to find the right business. What you are doing now is purely and simply not for you, Uke. People in the broadcasting industry know it. And in your heart you know it, too. You've got to get out. *Now.* Test yourself, even as you did in baseball; when you knew you stank and couldn't play you accepted the fact, hung around for years . . . unsung . . . a third-stringer, copying down Joe Garagiola's old jokes, trying to get a dry, understated delivery that would, from time to time, get you on the Carson show and would produce lower ratings than anyone else in the history of that show.

"Now is the time to face reality, because you're still young enough to get out. If it means unemployment for a year, two years, whatever, fine! You can surmount adversity. Remember, adversity is what produces character. Now you've got to take a whole new look at your life; who you are, where you're at, what you are all about. And when you deduce all of that you will find that you are NOTHING. You are all about NOTHING.

"I'm glad they are roasting you tonight, Uke. It's the right way to go out."

I can hear those words, or read them, and immediately tell you three things: He did it without notes. He did it in one take. He got as close to the bone as you can get—as Don Rickles and Jack Carter and the great insult artists have always done—without causing actual pain. He is brilliant.

We were doing a baseball telecast in Minneapolis once and at one point Howard used the word "truculent." He looked at me and said, "Obviously, you don't know what I am talking about." I said, "Sure I do. If you had a truck and I borrowed it, that would be a truck-you-lent." Howard waited a beat and said, "Need I say more?"

I will let you in on a secret. For all of his blather about the "tired litany of the ex-jocks," and his belief that the networks are too quick and eager to take them on, Cosell respects those who work at the craft. And, although the self-put-down is part of my style, I do work at mine. I prepare. On the air, I care about being right. I had everything to learn about voice and delivery and the technical side of broadcasting, and I spent ten years learning them. I didn't try to wisecrack my way through it.

And like Cosell, I am not afraid to be controversial. I was among the first to take a stand when the question arose of whether to admit women reporters into the locker rooms. The issue was clouded with passionate speeches about freedom of the press, the First Amendment, and equal rights.

Not many people wanted to tangle with the true, bedrock issue, which is: If you were a lady, and found yourself in a clubhouse with twenty-five naked guys, would you look?

As a personal matter, I favor admitting women sportswriters and sportcasters to the locker rooms. I can't think of any place that figures to be more instantly improved by a few whiffs of cologne. But I do suspect that the ladies get distracted, even though they insist that they need to be there to write their stories. Sometimes, when you read their articles the next day, in the middle of a word you will notice a capital letter.

Sure, I can understand why some of the players are embarrassed by having women around while they (the players) are undressed. I know when I'm working in the broadcasting booth, and I'm nude, I don't want strangers coming in there, either.

The transition from player to announcer was hard for me in only one respect. There is a great temptation, for a former player, to be overly critical of the athletes now on the field. I just have to watch myself. It would not be fair for me to expect these fellows to do things the way I did them. Not fair at all.

And that is why my role on the Monday night telecasts is so clearly defined. The other guys can get all excited about the home runs and no-hitters and triple plays. I'm the one who gets excited when the catcher holds on to a third strike—or the warmup tosses. If the catcher drops a pop foul, I'm the one who explains how he did it. I'm the only one who knows his frame of mind.

I am at my best on passed balls. I'm like the expert at a golf tournament, or a coach at halftime. I am able to diagram the play for the viewers.

Now back to you, Howard.

9. One Strike and We're All Out

IT WAS LIKE a variation of the question that George Patton once posed to his troops, and kids of a later generation asked their fathers: "What did you do in the war, Daddy?"

Only this time the question was: "What did you do during the strike?"

I heard it all over America in the midsummer of 1981. The stadiums were still idle when Johnny Carson, on the *Tonight Show,* asked me how I had been spending my time.

I told him I had planned to go back into the army. I figured I still owed them a few weeks, having gone AWOL in 1956 after a disagreement with my first sergeant during hand-grenade training. He wanted me to use a lob throw, the way they do in the movies. I preferred a baseball throw, which is more accurate and gets better distance. We argued and I went over the hill. And never went back.

Unfortunately, when I contacted my nearest army

recruiting office I learned that I had leave time coming, so I had to continue with my broadcasting.

Carson nodded and asked, "What are you going to do when you leave here?"

I said, "Tomorrow I'll be at Craters of the Moon, Idaho. I'm going around the country promoting un-sportsmanlike conduct school for kids. This is for youngsters in peewee football, basically. If the referee throws a flag, we encourage the kid to blow his nose on it and hand it back. Or they can slip a little Crazy Glue on the tip of his whistle and watch him pull his lip off."

Johnny did a double-take. *"Craters of the Moon, Idaho?"* he repeated.

The funny thing is, he thought I had made it up. But there really is such a town, at the foot of a volcano, just outside of Boise. It was the scene of the last major eruption in the United States prior to Mount St. Helens. When I was in Class C ball, our bus trips used to take us right by there, and the players would try to remember whose face the terrain reminded us of.

If the loss of eight weeks out of the 1981 season proved anything, it proved that baseball is as strong and elastic as ever. A strike nobody wanted was followed by a split-season plan that nobody seemed to like, and it all worked fine.

That hole in the middle of the schedule meant that there would be no twenty-game winners, and no hitters who drove in one hundred runs. But the teams came back to four new pennant races, and isn't that why God created September?

Like many fans, I had a sinking feeling that the rest of the season was going to be wiped out. In which case, these things would have happened:

—The company in the East that packs Delaware River mud into cans, to be used to rub the gloss off new baseballs, would have gone out of business (for years we have begged them to diversify).

—The sportswriters would have fanned out across the country, interviewing the players at their new jobs in feed stores and filling stations. They would have found Pete Rose on a sandlot in Philadelphia, crouched behind first base, waiting for a game to break out.

—With the billions saved by fans not buying tickets, parking their cars, or eating hot dogs, popcorn, and peanuts, the nation's economy might have turned around. People would have invested in the stock market or remodeled their homes. The rest would have gone into certificates of deposit.

It is a good thing the strike ended, after all. The longer it went on, the more people argued about it on radio call-in shows, and the harder the media tried to explain the issue, and the madder and more confused everybody got.

Both sides claimed that money was not the issue. The owners said they needed to be compensated, off the twenty-five-man roster, for a player lost to free agency. They needed this, they said, to protect the "competitive balance." The players said they liked the system the way it was. They were fighting, they said, to protect a right they had "won in court."

The issue was money. Since 1976, player salaries had tripled, thanks to the seven-figure, multi-year contracts the owners were tossing at so many free agents.

The compromise that ended the strike after fifty playing dates were canceled boiled down to this: The most a team can lose for signing a free agent is the twenty-fifth man on its roster. The fans really didn't care who won or who lost. The reaction of the fans was: Shut up and deal.

When the walkout began, I asked myself what I would have done if there had been a reason for striking when I was still a player, making my twenty grand or less? And there were probably a lot more reasons than there are now.

The players have a point when they ask why they should make life easier for the owners, just because the owners lack the discipline to do it themselves. On the other hand, it is pointless when the players say, as they have said repeatedly, "The owners wouldn't be paying those big salaries if they couldn't afford them." What has affording it got to do with anything? That is why credit cards were invented.

Given a choice between winning and running up costs, the owners unfailingly will choose to win. The need to win tops anything else that life can offer. They already know how it feels to be rich.

It is hard at this point to work up any sympathy for the players or the owners. When a utility infielder, or a pitcher who wins fourteen games, can sell himself for five hundred thousand dollars a year, even the players giggle softly. They also take the logical position that it isn't their duty to stop it.

If someone reminds them that they could kill the fowl that lays the golden egg, they are likely to shrug and respond, "The fowl will find a way to survive."

So the players want to keep the *status quo,* which, in the words of an old country preacher, is Latin for "de mess we is in." They like their freedom, their salaries, their thirty-five dollars a day in meal money. You give the average housewife thirty-five dollars a day and she will feed five people and have her hair done with the change.

An ex-player, who played for modest wages and probably got what he deserved, risks coming off like a sourbelly if he doesn't stand with the troops. But some of what the players say is wearing thin.

I heard Dave Parker, of the Pirates, tell an interviewer: "This game is harder than people think. Some days, we're out at the ball park eight or nine hours." An image of a pipefitter smashing his beer can through his TV screen came to mind.

After Andy Messersmith signed with Atlanta for a multi-year contract valued at a million and three-quarter dollars, a TV reporter asked why the negotiations had dragged out for months. "Was it just a matter of money," he asked, "or was there a principle involved?"

"Well," said the pitcher, "it started out as a money thing, but then it became a principle thing."

There was a kind of wild poetry to Andy's words. For most athletes today, the principle is clear: Grab it while you can. A career in pro sports is short, unlike that of a brain surgeon, or even a judge, who gets to sit down a lot.

A popular parlor game today is to wonder what players of the stature of Babe Ruth, Ty Cobb, Joe DiMaggio, or Ted Williams would bring in the current market. Clearly, Ruth would not receive a contract. He would get a partnership. As his widow once noted, "In my husband's day .280 hitters were not regarded as stars. They sat on the bench." I could have sat on the bench in Ruth's day, as easily as I did in my own.

In 1981, Dave Winfield, a lifetime .280 hitter, signed a ten-year contract with the New York Yankees said to be worth fifteen million dollars, not including bonus clauses. Winfield won his free agency after the San Diego Padre refused to meet his price or his personal demands. It was rumored that Dave wanted a veto in the event Ray Kroc, the McDonald's hamburger tycoon, decided to move the club. He also wanted a voice in team trades, more beef in the ground patties, and the right to change his name to Ronald McWinfield.

Do you remember when sports was the nation's escape from the hustle and bustle of everyday commerce? Now the athletes no longer merely sign contracts, they cut deals. The owners grumble, but pay, and some of them, such as George Steinbrenner and Ted Turner, don't even grumble. The players, of course, are having orgasms. Big money, rather than big performance, has created today's breed of superstar. When a streak hitter like Reggie Jackson can get a candy bar named after him, you conclude that the word "superstar" has been devalued. Or even the word "candy bar." Of course, I'm not jealous. I had one named after me, too. The Zero bar.

As a close observer of trends, I have kept myself prepared in the event of another strike. Radio stations recreated old games and newspapers ran old box scores during the last one. The owners missed an opportunity by not keeping the parks open and showing old baseball movies, such as *The Babe Ruth Story,* or *Pride of the Yankees,* or *The Winning Team,* which starred Ronnie Reagan.

I will continue to keep open as many options as I can. I still have several business ventures, including the various Bob Uecker academies. One is my famous Passed Ball School for kids. We teach young catchers how to miss the ball. I got the idea from people asking me what was the best way to catch a knuckleball. I told them that what worked for me was to wait for the ball to stop rolling, then just pick it up.

Of course, we also have adult education classes, such as our School for Tall-Building Climbers. I got this idea after two fellows climbed the World Trade Center in New York. The work is exciting, although I must admit that up to now our graduates have enjoyed very little success. Two of them failed to climb the C.N. Tower Building in Toronto, seventeen hundred feet high. We prefer that they start off with something smaller, such as a one-story building, or a Winnebago.

The most important warning we give our students, when they go through spring training, is: Don't touch the ledges! We consider this to be of life-and-death importance. There might be pigeon droppings on those ledges. The first time you grab the ledge, and you feel the pigeon droppings, your natural instinct is to say, "Aaagghh," and let go. And that is that.

During an earlier baseball strike—there have been three since 1972—I went into a sport fishing investment with my friend Al Hirt, the jazz trumpetist. We set up the company in a first-class way, printing a four-color brochure that showed Al floating in a swamp near New Orleans, with me sitting on top of his stomach with my feet in the water, and holding a rod.

I decided to back out of the deal after I found out how Al wanted to fish. One day we got into a boat and I looked around and didn't see any rods or reels, just a tackle box. He said not to worry about it. Fifteen miles out into the lake he cut off the motor, opened the tackle box and took out a stick of dynamite. I was appalled, having always considered myself a pretty good sportsman.

Jumbo, as his friends call him, lit the fuse and pitched the stick into the water. With his first cast we got about two hundred fish. After two or three more I said, "Look, I've had enough of this." With that he picked up another stick, lit the fuse, handed it to me and asked if I wanted to fish.

It was my only throw but I guess we got another one hundred fifty, and most of them were already cleaned. But that was the end of my sport fishing venture.

I hope there will never be another strike in baseball. But if there is, I won't be hurt. I can always go back into the service.

PART IV

Short Subjects

*In which he examines the mystique of
spring training, managers, umpires, and
the underworld of Little League.*

"Baseball owes me a lot. If I had to go into the tank to
lose a game, I would do it. I was not one of those
guys you had to go back two and three times to ask a
favor. And this is what I tell kids. You have to make
up your mind sooner or later, do you want to be good,
or do you want to be a tanker?"

10. It Happens Every Spring

"WELCOME TO DIAMOND THREE, men. During your stay here you will be taught the art of fighting snakebite, how to survive for days without water, and how to extract water from the cactus plants behind second base. You will never see people out here. You will learn not to care when dirt gets in your bubble gum. And you will be given a chance to play baseball at its very worst. Welcome to Diamond Three, men."

Okay, so it won't make the world forget General George Patton's speech to the troops on the eve of D-Day. But this was my welcome each spring to the other scrubs, in my role as honorary captain of the irregulars, with the Braves, the Cardinals, and the Phillies.

Spring training was my favorite part of the baseball season. One year, with the Phillies, I took a call in the clubhouse. Hanging up the phone, I turned to the fellows around me and said, casually, "It was my wife. She wanted to know where I've been all winter."

They call it the Dreamer's Month. In March, on paper,

every team looks stronger than it did a year ago, and they are counting heavily on a player they got in a trade with a team that no longer wanted him.

It's the same every year. The rituals never vary. A pitcher may have nothing more on the ball than the autograph of the league president, but in March they all look like the reincarnation of Walter Johnson.

In short, spring training is a fantasy land, a place where rookies with rheumatism hit .400 and the ball *sounds* louder, whether it is off the bat or landing ka-pow in the catcher's glove. Reality doesn't sink in until mid-April is on the calendar.

Even the managers can sometimes suspend their critical judgment. In places like Bradenton and Orlando, West Palm Beach and Phoenix, they say to themselves, "Well, we all start even, and why shouldn't it be me this year?"

They also tell each other things like: "So help me, Max, this kid could be another DiMaggio. His name is Higgins or Hawkins, I'm not sure which, but he's sensational . . . gawd, if he could only hit."

Many people have the impression that players in the spring stay on a pretty tough schedule. The first two weeks are the worst. The pitchers and the catchers have it harder than anybody. They pitchers have to run, run, run. The catchers never get a break. You have to stick around until everyone is finished throwing. Or throwing up.

Anybody could do it.

Actually, the biggest setback the American players ever suffered was when the Japanese teams began making occasional visits to Florida. You get an idea of how well-conditioned the American baseball player is when you see a runner in June try for three bases. No sight is more pathetic, no effort sorrier, than the spectacle of a baseball player legging out a triple.

Sliding into the bag, he calls time for the ostensible purpose of dusting off his uniform. But he is so pooped, so exhausted, that you begin to think that his next move is to call in the paramedics.

By contrast, the Japanese go to something that resembles a Marine boot camp. They scale mountains, run obstacle courses and climb ropes.

At major-league training camps in the U.S., the players will touch their toes, run a little and then play golf, unless they prefer to go fishing. Fishing will give a man a hell of a workout, especially if he gets a bite every three hours.

A majority of the players manage to avoid the Spartan existence of camp life itself. They bring along their families, renting places on the sands of Vero Beach and St. Petersburg—or, if they are based on the desert, they occupy an oasis with pools at Scottsdale, Arizona.

The Japanese player, summoned for reville at six in the morning, will go for his bowl of rice under a thatched roof before he is asked to take a run up Mt. Fuji. This is an athlete lean and hard, and ready to leg out a triple.

For me, personally, the great thing about spring training was working on my tan. When the weather was bad I would just get liquored up and do a handstand and bring a flush to my face. Works almost as well.

It used to be, in the days before football and basketball were played twelve months a year, and golf and tennis players were not yet let in through the front door of the country club, that sports fans had little to do but wait for the start of spring training. There were always those first exciting clues that told us the season was just around the corner.

You would see a page-one photograph of a few early arrivals doing sit-ups or hopscotching their way through a broken field of old tires, or two guys throwing a medicine ball at each other's stomachs, a fairly decent target at that stage of training.

Of course, from my own experience I can tell you that those photographs were usually faked. In all probability, the ball wasn't even a medicine ball. More likely it was a rubber beach ball and a photographer borrowed it from a little kid at the going rate of twenty-five cents an hour.

No doubt the players tossed it around for a total of five minutes, at which point they noticed the sun was out and retired to the clubhouse for a beer.

All of which goes to the very heart of what spring training is all about. Traditionally, baseball players have never deliberately built a muscle in their lives. They have believed that either you had muscles or you didn't. March was a month to get the old timing and coordination down pat, and to prepare your *head*. Once you were in the right frame of mind to open the season, why, your body had no choice but to go along.

If nothing else, spring training is a rich and bottomless source of stories that reflect the romance and character of the sport. In a less frantic age, the teams traveled by train, and the players had time to talk about the sport and to agitate each other and concoct all kinds of wild schemes. They would do this traveling north out of Florida, with the countryside flashing by the window. The scenery, it should be noted, is not particularly absorbing, unless you happen to be attracted to cabbage palms and slash pines.

So the boys would sit around thinking up subjects to argue about, and this led naturally enough to a lot of enduring tales. One of them concerns the grizzled old catcher, Clint Courtney, known in the pits as Scrap Iron.

In his salad days, Courtney caught for the old Washington Senators, and one spring he promoted a footrace between Pedro Ramos, his battery mate, and Don Hoak of the Cincinnati Reds.

The teams were barnstorming through the South together, and the players entered into one of those club-car arguments about who was faster, Ramos or Hoak.

Ramos was then a skinny young pitcher who could fly, but nobody realized it because he did not know how to get off to a proper start. And, besides, he seldom got a base hit. Courtney baited the Cincinnati players by claiming that, "Anybody beats my man, he's got to put his feet down real regular."

So they decided to hold the race before a game in Chattanooga at one hundred yards. The guys on both clubs started making bets, and on the way north Courtney would stroll through the Reds' part of the train hustling bets that would be covered by the Washington players. Altogether, the pot was rumored to have reached seven thousand dollars.

The day before the race, Courtney received permission to go on ahead of the clubs to set up the racing course at the Chattanooga ball park. The players arrived in a state of great excitement, and everyone lined up along the way, most of them near the finish line.

At the starting point, Hoak crouched in the accepted American track stance, while Ramos was standing up with his arms dangling at his sides. As everyone expected, Hoak got off on top. He quickly opened a lead of about five yards, and then—as Courtney told it—here came Pedro Ramos.

He cut the margin down gradually, caught Hoak, then

won it pulling away. Ramos beat him by about ten yards, to the utter amazement of the Cincinnati players.

They paid off, and some of them probably do not know to this day that Clint Courtney's course measured *one hundred and twenty yards*.

The phrase "It happens every spring" wasn't invented to describe the craziness and mass optimism that grips baseball at that special time of the year, but it fits as snugly as a catcher's mask.

In the spring, even the writers are easily spoiled and tend to be temperamental. Chicago scribes are the treasurers of a classic story that dates back to when big-league teams moved like wrestlers from town to town, picking up expense money as they headed north to open the season.

The hero of this story is T-Bone Otto, a legendary Chicago scribe who was covering the White Sox on a tour across West Texas. The White Sox had played the Giants in a town called Alpine, and after finishing his account of the game, T-Bone Otto turned upstream in search of refreshments.

He looked all over town, a task that didn't consume a great deal of time, and found every eatery shut as tight as the lid on a jar of bees. When he returned to his hotel, grouchy and thirsty and hungry, he was informed that the White Sox had just purchased the contract of Willie Kamm, an infielder of some promise. He sat down at his typewriter and pounded out a story that began:

"ALPINE—In this lousy little Texas town, where a man can't get anything to eat after 9:00 P.M., the White Sox today acquired Willie Kamm."

Of course, a fellow doesn't have to be clairvoyant to

guarantee that certain things will happen every spring, such as:

—A manager who has no one else to play the position will announce, dramatically, that a certain rookie has the job until he loses it.

—The players who grumble the most about how hard they are working will sneak away after a game to play eighteen holes of golf.

—At least one player will be laid up with a serious sunburn.

—A guy who never hit over .220 in his life will say that this year he is going to wait for his pitch.

—No matter how homely the waitress in the motel coffee shop is, she will get a big play from the single players if she owns a car.

—Every manager will say at least once in every interview that, "You can always use another pitcher."

—An actor will put on a uniform and work out with the Dodgers.

—A player who was traded from a contender to a last-place team will be quoted as saying that he is glad to be with a team that wants him.

—The manager of a second-division club will predict that his team will be improved. (He will be fired in August by the general manager who put the team together.)

—George Steinbrenner will make headlines by criticizing his manager, another owner, one or more of his players, or all of these.

—Billy Martin will make headlines by getting into a fight, or by not getting into a fight.

—Yogi Berra will be credited with a funny remark that was originally uttered by a nightclub comedian.

—A sports columnist will warn that salaries have

gotten so out of line, the fans are being turned off, and the sport is in danger of dying. (A new attendance record will be set.)

—A star player will not report to camp, threatening to retire unless his contract is renegotiated. Both sides will wind up happy. The club will announce that it did not renegotiate the contract, which would have set a poor precedent, but merely extended the contract at a slightly higher figure. The player will have missed the first week or two of camp, the most boring part.

It was a matter of pride with some players never to report to camp on time. Mike Marshall, the great relief pitcher who had his finest years with the Dodgers and the Expos, was always working toward another degree in college, and usually showed up around St. Patrick's Day to chase the snakes out of Florida.

My old friend Richie Allen sometimes arrived on schedule, then quickly disappeared for several days to have his eyes checked, or to go visit a sick horse.

One of the masters of this art was the colorful Orestes (Minnie) Minoso, who held out not for financial gain, but because he loved his native Cuba and preferred to stay there as late as possible in the spring. Once, reporting five days late to the Cleveland camp, he was met by an irritated Hank Greenberg, then the general manager of the Indians.

"Suppose," Hank asked Minoso, "you were in my position?"

"You mean if I Greenberg and you Minnie?" asked Minoso.

"Exactly," said Greenberg.

Minoso smiled. "I pat you on back and I say, 'Minnie, you good boy, you fine fellow, you hustle all the time. All right if you take off four-five days."

• • •

As a player, I always went to spring training in Florida, where the early weather was often so cool and so wet that the newspapers had to use pictures of last year's bathing beauties dipping their toes into the Atlantic.

There is always a basic conflict in the spring between management and the players. The management prefers an environment that is almost hermetically sealed, and goes to great lengths to keep the players away from the nearest beach, fearing that such a place offers too much in the way of temptations. The players complain that there are never enough temptations.

I can assure you that both complaints are justified.

One of the things I hated most about spring training was the long bus rides starting at 5:00 A.M. to play another team across the state. As they say, everything gets easier with practice except getting up in the morning. I would never recommend to anyone getting up before dawn to drive to a spring training game between say, the Braves and the Red Sox. Still, it might be worth doing once. You would remember it a long time, and that would save having to do it again.

But it really boils down to keeping things in perspective.

Once, we headed out of our camp at West Palm Beach to play a B game against the Twins at Orlando. We followed the coastal highway to the Astronaut trail, until our bus took us past the launching pad at what was then Cape Kennedy.

Poised like a great white bullet on the gantry was the rocket that would carry the crew of one of the Apollo flights toward the moon. The bus grew quiet. All of those aboard swung their eyes to the window and stared out through the early-morning mist, across the Banana River, at the huge ship visible through the wispy clouds like the first glimpse of the mountain Bali H'ai, in the movie *South Pacific*.

Finally, the silence was broken. From the back of the bus came the voice of one of the players. "Gee," he said, "it makes our B team game with the Twins seem almost insignificant."

11. The Fearless Leaders

DO YOU HAVE trouble keeping track of which manager is with which team, and who was there before him? Of course you do. It is like trying to understand the price index on pork futures. It is even more confusing than keeping up with the ex-husbands of the wife of New York's Governor Carey. It makes your eyeballs burn.

In 1961, Phil Wrigley, the reclusive owner of the Chicago Cubs, decided to try a perfectly bold experiment. He decided not to have any manager at all. Instead, he appointed what he called a board of rotating coaches, six of them, each to take his turn at the helm of the team for a period of weeks.

The experiment ended in 1963, after it had become apparent that the Cubs played just as miserably without a manager as they did with one, and thus were deprived of someone to take most of the blame.

Charley Metro happened to be the coach-of-the-month during a game in 1962, when he was ejected for arguing with an umpire. At that moment, Joey Amalfitano, an infielder with Houston, jumped out of the visitors' dugout, pointed to the Chicago coaches sitting in a row, and shouted across the field: "Okay, each of you guys move up one seat!"

I played under six different managers in my six years in the big leagues: Birdie Tebbetts, Johnny Keane, Red Schoendienst, Gene Mauch, Bobby Bragan and Luman Harris. They were an interesting cross-section. Tebbetts was warm, outgoing, fatherly, quick with a funny line. Mauch was smart, hot-tempered, always trying to stay three innings ahead of the other guy. He surprised me one night, when I saw him quietly holding hands with his wife in a hotel lobby during spring training.

Keane was a gentle, proud man, who had spent his life in the minors, whose playing career was ended by a beanball, who managed farm clubs for twenty years and had one year of glory, when the Cardinals won the pennant for him in 1964.

Red Schoendienst had been a championship player in Milwaukee and St. Louis. He was no back-slapper, but he was businesslike and fair. Bragan had the look of a bartender in a Gay Nineties saloon; he smoked cigars, played the piano, liked a good laugh. Luman Harris had pitched for Connie Mack, was tough but not threatening.

All of them had one thing in common. All of them, sooner or later, would get fired.

You conclude that it takes a special kind of rainbow chaser to want to be a baseball manager. When Dave Bristol was hired in Atlanta, a reporter asked if he considered himself a fiery type of manager. "I guess so," he replied, "I've been fired three times." Later, he moved on to the Giants, and was fired a fourth time.

Do you know what the average tenure is among big-league managers? Two and a half years. Migrant fruit picking is more secure than that.

You begin to get the idea that the best way to get a manager's job is to be delivering bottled water to the team's office at the moment the last one is getting fired.

When Gil Hodges was named the manager of the Washington Senators, his old Dodger boss, Walter Alston, was asked for his reaction. "I'm happy for him," said Alston, "that is, if you think becoming a big-league manager is a good thing to have happen to you."

Hodges inherited a last-place team in Washington. One night, after another loss, Frank Slocum, a former newsman who had worked in the commissioner's office, stood in his doorway. "The Dodgers just released Gino Cimoli," said Slocum, mentioning a former Hodges teammate, and an outfielder of average talents.

Wearily, Hodges looked up from his desk. "Why are you telling me this?" he asked.

"I thought he might be able to help you," replied Slocum.

"Frank," said Hodges, "did it ever occur to you that if I thought Gino Cimoli could help this club, I'd quit right now?"

No one in America is second-guessed more often, or hears more unwanted advice, than the manager of a big-league baseball team. And that includes the President, plumbers, and producers of X-rated movies.

The fact is, one manager in twenty can influence a team emotionally. Technically, in terms of the moves that are open to him, a manager can win or lose—actually decide the outcome—of possibly eight to ten games a year, tops.

When a team finishes poorly, and elects to bring in a new field leader without making any serious roster

changes, it is doing just one thing. It is grandstanding for
the fans, saying to them: "Your good ownership is doing
something, trying to bring you, our deserving fans, a
winner."

Richie Allen used to say that the public is mistaken
when it believes that managers are fired. "They aren't
fired," said Richie, "they are only moved, like players.
If you want to say that managers are fired, then I've been
fired four times." That is a new but not unreasonable
way to look at the practice of teams' hiring managers
who have been fired elsewhere, usually more than once.

Considering the nature of the job, and the insecurity of
it, you tend to ask yourself why any sane person would
pursue this line of work. The answer is twofold. First,
the job satisfies the power needs that exist in most of us.
A manager controls twenty-five men, plus a staff. His
words are recorded by press, radio, and television. His
friendship and company are sought by important people,
at least while he remains on the job.

What else could the average manager do that would
pay as well and be as exciting? They will tell you that it
beats operating a crane, driving a bread truck or selling
jock-straps.

Yet the pressure of the job changes them as people.
Even playful, fun-loving types like Bobby Bragan and
Luman Harris became more serious and touchy and less
approachable.

With a few exceptions, they turn into people you have
trouble recognizing. Of course, Walter Alston stayed the
same: quiet, aloof, steady as a rock. Casey Stengel was
nutty and lovable when he won, more so when he lost.
And nothing will ever change Billy Martin. He was a
tough s.o.b. when he played and when he managed and
he will still be on the day he dies. And I love him for it.

I was fond of Bobby Bragan and I still am. He had a great sense of humor. But he was more fun to be around when he was a coach than when the Braves hired him as their manager.

The first thing Bobby did when we returned to Milwaukee after spring training was go out to the bullpen and tear down a kind of recreation room the boys had created out there. We had taken wire clippers and cut out part of a snow fence and made an area for ourselves. We built a table, suspended it from under the stands, and arranged several boxes and crates so you could play cards and eat. The little guy who drove the scooter to the pitcher's mound was named George, and we would bribe him with a dozen baseballs and have a steady supply of hot dogs or bratwurst or whatever we wanted.

Bragan knew about the arrangement from his days as a bullpen coach with Houston. So he had everything ripped out and fired poor George. Bobby, Bobby. Where did we go wrong?

The year before, when Bragan was a coach, the hot-foot was just epidemic in baseball. Players would be sitting on the bench, watching the game, and you would crawl from one end of the dugout to the other, sticking matches in their shoes and lighting them, and then see those feet go up like someone running the keyboard on a piano.

Inevitably, the action got more complicated. Guys would smoke a cigarette down to about a half inch and stick it in your belt loop—even while you were on the field. I looked up one time and our second baseman was out in the field, beating out flames on his uniform.

The planning was elaborate, like spies preparing to blow up a factory. One trick was to chew a stick of gum, then press it against the side of the victim's shoe. You could just touch the cigarette but to the gum and it would hold. When the cigarette burned down far enough, it would go right through the leather, and the poor fellow couldn't get his shoe off fast enough.

Or someone would light your shoelaces. All of a sudden your shoes split right down the middle and the laces were gone. It was just one piece of nonsense after another.

One day the Houston team came into County Stadium, and Turk Farrell found me before the game. He said, "Uke, bring some lighter fluid out to the bullpen." I said, "Whaddya gonna do?" He said, "Just bring it. We're gonna torch Bragan."

I gave Farrell a can of fluid and he stashed it under the bench in the visitors' bullpen. When the game started Bragan sat down and kept his eyes on the field. I was leaning as far over the rail of our bullpen as I could. When I saw what Farrell was doing I couldn't believe it. He took the cap off the can and sprayed it up and down Bragan's shoes and pants legs. Then he took a match and threw it on him. Poof! Bragan did the damndest dance I have ever seen. Chief Nok-a-homa, the Indian who sat out in the teepee and did a few war whoops whenever the Braves homered, would have been proud.

Bragan was a product of the Branch Rickey system with the old Brooklyn Dodgers, and had come up through their farm clubs. He could really get on your case. He had a way of talking out of the side of his mouth, like Humphrey Bogart, and he could dust you off equally well with a sarcastic line or with your basic seaman's vocabulary.

One day, after the Braves had moved to Atlanta, the team was in a wretched slump, and Bobby and Del Crandall had gotten into a shouting match at the end of a road trip. So Bobby decided to call a clubhouse meeting to clear the air. He just started moving from locker to locker, and as he faced each player he would curl his lip and say, "Bleep you." And on to the next one.

Finally, he was a few feet away from Eddie Mathews, who seldom made trouble, but didn't suffer insults, real or imagined, lightly. When Bobby got to him, Eddie's fists were curled. Bragan paused, looked at his eyes, said nothing, and moved on to the next locker. No one ever accused Bragan of being stupid.

Each manager loses in his own way. Sometimes, in his own several ways. Some swear, some sulk, some suffer in silence. When Alvin Dark managed the Giants, he once picked up a clubhouse stool and threw it against a wall, unfortunately catching a finger in a hinge and ripping off the tip of it. When he showed up in a bandage the next day, the players started calling him "Lefty." Alvin also quoted the Bible a lot.

Silent, stern Walter Alston once stopped a bus and challenged his entire team to a fistfight.

After his New York Mets lost a doubleheader, one of the games in twenty-three innings, Casey Stengel took off his clothes, stood in the middle of the locker room, and leaped straight in the air. When heads swiveled in his direction, he shrugged and said, "I just wanted to see if I was still alive."

And when Fred Hutchinson was managing the Reds, teams that followed them into a town could always tell if the Reds had lost by the number of light bulbs and chairs that had been smashed in the visitors' clubhouse.

In my time, the manager who was most respected by the players was Hutchinson. The one we most liked to be around was Stengel, and the one we most liked to analyze was Gene Mauch.

Eddie Kasko was with the Cardinals in 1957 when Hutch was the manager there, and pushing the Braves for first place. "He sent up Del Ennis to pinch-hit one night in a tight spot," recalled Kasko, "and Ennis had that real big bat—the U-1 model. He swung at a two-and-oh pitch and popped it up.

"Coming back to the dugout, he was swinging that bat like a cane, walking along in that slow, shuffling sort of walk that he had. You could see that Hutch was seething, and he was trying hard to control himself.

"Just as Ennis stepped down into the dugout, he flung his bat toward the bat rack, and out of the corner of his eye Hutch saw it go by. He wheeled around and grabbed it and, man, you should have seen the players on the Cardinal bench scatter. Hutch took the bat and began beating it against those concrete steps.

"Then he threw it to the floor and began stomping on it, and you know what? The damned thing wouldn't break. Finally, Hutch picked it up and gently handed it back to Ennis. 'Here,' he said, 'keep it. It has good wood in it.'"

Fred Hutchinson was the hero of some of baseball's favorite essays on fury and indignation. In his time he wrecked more chairs than Duncan Phyfe built. He was seldom misunderstood. He was never patronizing, not to his players or to the batboy or to reporters, not necessarily in order of importance. He was a big bear of a man, restless, with curly hair and sad eyes. He was not a phrasemaker, but he had the knack of saying a lot in a small space.

In the winter before the pennant race of 1964—that great race between the Cards, the Reds, and the

Phillies—the story broke that Hutch was ill with cancer. It was in June that the word spread that he was dying. We heard it from the Cincinnati players. "He started to smoke again and to take an occasional drink," said one. "He knew he wasn't going to whip it and he figured, what the hell, he might as well do the things he enjoyed doing."

He turned the team over to Dick Sisler in August. He would still visit the ball park and his picture would be in the paper the next day. His friends winced at the photographs of the drawn, gaunt face.

He was in the clubhouse on the last day of the season, the day the Reds lost the pennant. Dick Sisler nodded in his direction and told reporters: "I'm only sorry we couldn't have won it for that gentleman there."

Hutchinson overheard him. "I'm only sorry," he said, "they couldn't have won it for themselves."

I never played under Casey Stengel, but I played against him, and I am reasonably sure we would have gotten along. I can still see Casey marching out to the mound with his hands jammed in his back pockets, or punching the air with a fist in the dugout, or sprawled on the bench like Cleopatra on a barge, regaling his writers.

It was a tossup whether Stengel's most memorable achievement was winning ten pennants with the Yankees, or finishing tenth three times with the Mets, and making them the greatest failure story in history.

He had one of those rubbery faces that make a fellow look as if he could swallow his nose. His legs were so lumpy it looked as though he were smuggling walnuts in his stockings. The week that Casey retired from the Mets, at seventy-four, *Look* magazine ran a picture of him stalking away from some umpires after arguing about a call. The umpires were all laughing.

In his heyday with the Mets, Casey came to Florida one spring with his hair dyed a strange, youthful shade of henna. It was a wild sight, that hair, above that wrinkled, cartoon face. The Mets players could hardly wait to tell you about it.

"Have you seen Casey?" they braced each visitor. "He looks like Dorian Gray's UNCLE."

He had his faults. He could be rough and impatient with young players, and cruel in his opinions. Of Jimmy Piersall, who had a history of odd behavior, he said: "He's great, but you gotta play him in a cage." Bobby Richardson was straight as an arrow, and Casey didn't know what to make of it: "He doesn't smoke, doesn't drink, doesn't run around with girls and doesn't stay out late, and he still can't hit .250."

But Stengel believed in the miracle of being young. "I'll tell you about youth," he said. "Look how big it is. They break a record every day."

I especially liked what he said when he turned eighty-one, and a reporter asked what his plans were. "To tell you the truth," he said, "what I'd like to become is an astronaut."

12. The Men in Blue

MANY YEARS AGO, when the world was young, an umpire named Jocko Conlan called a strike on Richie Ashburn, a career .300 hitter then with the Phillies.

"Where was that pitch?" Ashburn snarled, in the ballplayers' traditional retort to a call that went against them.

Conlan, who had the look of a leprechaun, did not answer, at least not directly. What he said was, "Okay, *you* umpire. *You* call the next pitch."

Ashburn, startled, never moved his bat as the next one popped into the catcher's mitt. Over his shoulder, he peeked at Jocko and said, tentatively, "Strike?"

Obligingly, Jocko threw up his right hand and called a strike. Then he marched out and dusted off home plate and finally poked a finger in Ashburn's chest. "Richie," he said, "you have just had the only chance a hitter has ever had in the history of baseball to bat and umpire at the same time. And you blew it."

Sports is not a perfect society, so the day is still distant when it will be run on an honor system in which the players call their own pitches. In fact, the 1979 baseball season, when the regular umpires went on strike, may be as close as we ever get.

Let's face it. Umpiring is not an easy or a happy way to make a living. In the abuse they suffer, and the pay they get for it, you see an imbalance that can only be explained by their need to stay close to a game they an't resist. They are like the fellow who cleans up after the elephants at the circus, and whose complaints are greeted with the suggestion that he quit. "What?" he replies, "and give up show business?"

The sad truth is that baseball has never shown a great deal of heart in its treatment of the veteran umpires. The minimum pay for that position is $17,500, rising to a top of around forty grand. Some players probably pay their tailor more than most big-league umpires make.

You picture an ump walking to the mound when Nolan Ryan or Tommy John or Phil Niekro is pitching, and they turn their backs and tell him to leave a message with their answering service.

Clearly, the umpires feel underpaid in a job that requires them to make judgments on performers earning up to a million dollars a year. Their expenses are high. They accept insults as a matter of course. Injuries are common. Crowds are seldom more amused than when an umpire gets hit by a foul tip on an important part of his body.

And the life they lead is so lonely, they are never in danger of running into Margaret Trudeau or Bianca Jagger. They do not mingle with the players, fly on the same plane, or sleep in the same hotels.

Meanwhile, ballplayers collect thirty-three dollars a day for meals alone, and most of them sleep until noon.

Insulting the umpire is a pastime as old as baseball itself. In organized baseball's first recorded game, in 1846, a New York player named Davis was fined six cents for cussing the ump.

It was Tom Gorman, among the best of my time, who spoke for all the men in blue when he said: "Nobody ever says anything nice about an umpire, unless it's when he dies and then somebody writes in the paper, 'he was a good umpire.' Oh, once in a while a player will tell you that you worked a good game behind the plate, but when that happens, it's always the winning pitcher who says it."

Yet the umpires have a special role in the structure of baseball. To many fans, their lasting image of the sport is the Norman Rockwell drawing of the four umpires huddled under an umbrella, one holding out his hand, testing for rain.

At one time the top names in umpiring was Paparella, Passarella, Donatelli, Dascoli, Guglielmi and Secory. All of which moved Walker Cooper, the hard-bitten Cardinal catcher of the 1940s, to a wry complaint. "Every guy that gets off the boat," said Cooper, "has an indicator in his hand."

Mostly they were frustrated players who never got beyond the low minors. Today they are more likely to be the products of umpiring schools, who paid their dues in the college, amateur and minor-league ranks.

My impression is that umpires today are regarded with more respect than in the past, and television is at least partly responsible. Instant replays have supported their decisions a dramatically high percentage of the time.

The good ones last twenty years or more, and it helps if they have a sense of humor, and a little discretion. "Sometimes," I once heard Tom Gorman say, "when a game gets close and tempers are short, you hear things from the dugout and you holler at 'em to shut up, and if they don't you walk over to the bench. Now, when you've committed yourself that far, you gotta chase somebody. You don't want to hurt the club so you pick maybe a guy who pitched the day before and isn't gonna be called on again that day.

"So one particular day in Ebbets Field I'm gettin' it pretty good from the Dodger bench, and I finally walk over there and somebody has to go. So I point in just a general direction and I say, 'Yer outta here, John Van Cuyk,' because he'd pitched yesterday, you see, and I'm doing them a favor.

"Chuck Dressen is managing in Brooklyn then and he says, 'Who you want out?' And I repeat, 'Van Cuyk.' and Chuck says, 'That's great, but you'll have to yell a little louder because I sent him back to the Texas League last night.'"

On another occasion, Gorman was umpiring a game involving Leo Durocher's New York Giants. It so happened that Tom called a close play at first base against the Giants, and Durocher stormed out of the dugout and demanded: "Why, Tom, why?"

To distract him, Gorman said the first thing that came into his mind, which was: "Your first baseman had the wrong foot on the bag."

Well, that stopped Leo, and he went back to the dugout, trying to decide for himself just exactly what went wrong in his argument with Gorman. Then it dawned on him, and he rushed back out to the field. "Look, Tom," he said, "you've been umpiring in the big leagues for five or six years now. You mean to tell me that nobody ever told you that it didn't make any difference which foot the first baseman has on the bag?"

As a class, umpires are tireless storytellers, and one of the best was Jocko Conlan, who was five-seven, left-handed, and as Irish as Finian's Rainbow. Jocko added a lot of rich pages to baseball's anthology of humor. Some of his National-League squabbles with Frank Frisch and Leo Durocher were like vaudeville acts. He threw them out of the games many times, but only for just cause.

Once, when Frisch was managing the Pirates against the Giants on a stifling day in the Polo Grounds, he called for time and walked down to home plate from the third-base coaching box. "Jocko," asked Frank, "put me out of the game."

"What for?" asked Conlan.

"Because," said Frisch, "I can't stand this heat and I can't stand those .225 hitters I got. Besides, my feet are killing me. I want to go home and sit by my petunias."

Conlan, honorable man that he was, refused.

The first time I ever met Jocko, he called a strike on me and I stepped out of the box, making small animal noises. "That was no strike," I moaned.

"The next one is," he said, mildly.

I don't remember whether it was or not, but I swung anyway. You didn't take chances with Jocko.

One of Jocko's fondest memories was of the day he outsmarted a bloodthirsty crowd at Ebbets Field. It so happened that Bobby Bragan, who later managed the Braves, was then a young catcher for the Dodgers, and he was on first base when Pete Reiser tried to stretch a double with two out against the Chicago Cubs.

Reiser was out on a close play at third, and since the slower Bragan had not yet crossed the plate Conlan ruled that the Dodger run didn't count. Durocher charged out of the Dodger dugout and kicked dirt on Jocko's pants. Jocko kicked back. Beer bottles began to fly.

"Get out to second base or you'll be killed," yelled Charlie Grimm, the manager of the Cubs, but Jocko stood his ground. Police finally quieted the crowd.

After the game, the police wanted to give Jocko an escort to the nearest subway, but he felt that such a move would only encourage more serious fan reaction. So, suddenly, a man stepped through the exit gate from Ebbets Field wearing a tan suit, straw hat, bow tie, and two-toned shoes. It was Conlan, who walked safely past a mob of three thousand fans, looking for a guy in a blue suit.

Jocko had a temper you could fry fish on. He was unorthodox in his approach to his profesion. No one could ever say of Jocko that he didn't want to become involved. If Charlie Dressen had listened to him in 1951, Bobby Thomson might never have hit that historic home run for the Giants. As Dressen motioned to his bullpen, Jocko shook his head. "You're bringing in what? Branca? A fast-ball pitcher?"

Years later, Dressen did listen to him. In Milwaukee, Charlie was about to remove pitcher Bob Hendley. Jocko wandered out to the mound. "Whaddya wanta make a change for?" he asked. "He's pitching good." The astonished Dressen listened, and maybe, just maybe, he remembered that fateful day at the Polo Grounds in 1951. Charlie changed his mind. Hendley stayed in the game and threw a shutout.

13. Big League, Little League

I AGREE WITH Yogi Berra, who once said that Little League baseball is a very good thing because it keeps the parents off the streets.

Sure, parents get in the way. That's why they're parents. But as a father of a former Little-Leaguer, I think there are a number of things you can do to help your youngster if he is not in the starting lineup. You can invite the kid who is playing in front of him over to your house the night before a game, and serve him a rotten meal. Or you can volunteer to drive the car pool that day, and just not bother to pick that boy up.

Listen, it is hard not to get involved when your child is out there, fulfilling your hopes and dreams. My youngest son was the one who took after me. I was proud of him. In their championship game one year he struck out three times. And in the final inning, with the bases loaded, he let a ground ball go right through his legs to let in the winning run.

It was a great feeling for me, and I know he felt the

same way, as we walked to our car together while the other parents threw eggs and garbage at us and broke in our windshield.

If you don't care to take the game quite so seriously, that attitude is all right, too. You have to remember what the country was like before we had Little Leagues. Berra, the great Yankee catcher, who later managed the Yankees and the Mets, recalled: "When I was a kid we didn't have no lighted stadiums. We didn't always have nine to a side. We'd play with four kids, two on a side, and sometimes if we had only three we made that do, too. One would pitch, one hit and one shag. We'd do it for hours."

Possibly the greatest tribute ever paid to Little League baseball came in September of 1964, in Houston, on a night when the Phillies were in the process of blowing a pennant. A baby-faced rookie named Joe Morgan had beaten the Phillies with a bloop single in the last of the ninth. By the time Gene Mauch, the manager of the Phillies, got to the locker room he found several of his players bellying up to the buffet table, stuffing their faces.

"WE GOT BEAT," screamed Mauch, "by a guy who looks LIKE A LITTLE-LEAGUER." So saying, and with a mighty sweep of his arm, Mauch cleared the table. Barbecued spareribs, cold cuts, watermelon slices, potato salad all went flying, spattering the street clothes hanging in the nearest lockers. "Boy," said one player, "the food sure goes fast around here."

Let me assure you, there is nothing wrong in being a Little-Leaguer or even looking like one. The endurance of the sport depends on the very young.

On his last visit to Yankee Stadium, his voice reduced to a hoarse whisper by the cancer that was killing him,

Babe Ruth urged the parents of the country, "Start him when he's young, teach him to play baseball when he's four years old." How Babe arrived at that age isn't clear, but no doubt he just considered three to be too immature.

When Ty Cobb, his own days numbered, took a final look around him at the game he loved, he, too, made a plea to young America: "Boys," he said, "strive to master the lost arts of a great game. Unless you dedicate yourself to that task now, as the old-timers die off one by one, they will have vanished forever."

Ruth and Cobb and the guardians of the game knew something the critics cannot understand: that there was never a game more ideally suited than baseball to the soaring spirit, the boundless energy of the eternal child. "With a bat and a ball and his imagination," Branch Rickey once said, "a boy is a complete team."

Today, of course, Rickey would have amended that statement to read, "a boy . . . or a girl . . ."

No one ever spoke more lyrically about the game than Rickey, the man who invented the farm system, discovered Dizzy Dean, brought Jackie Robinson across the color line and never took a drink in his life, even though he once managed the St. Louis Browns. Rickey understood kids and knew why they were important to baseball. He also knew why baseball was important to them. "Leisure is wonderful in creative hands," he said. "It accounts for great architecture, great paintings, and great music. Leisure, however, is a damnable thing in the hands of an adolescent."

Added Rickey: "Baseball is a romance that begins when a boy is very young; it brings a diamond into his vision where the bases are fixed and the outfield is endless."

My own four kids—Leann, Steve, Sue Ann and

Bobby—grew up around ball parks. Like all kids, they had their heroes. After every game they wanted to go home with a different player.

When I was a preteen, we made do with a lump of something that passed for a baseball, and maybe a broom handle for a bat. We could always get up a game and there was never a problem finding a vacant lot—Rickey's endless outfield. In the forties and early fifties, America was still rich in vacant lots, the diamonds of our boyhood dreams. The great urban problems, the crisis of the inner cities to come, would change all that.

Today it is far easier to find a mini-stadium than a vacant lot. Kids thrive on the scale-model big-league world around them: bleachers, scoreboards, press boxes, p.a. systems. They cultivate the mannerisms . . . the tap of the bat to knock dirt off rubber-cleated shoes, hitching the belt, rubbing rosin on their hands, spitting bubble-gum juice across the plate.

I have no interest in getting into the question of whether Little-League baseball does more good than harm, if there is such a question. I like what Doug Rader, who played third base for Houston and San Diego, once said about his boyhood in Northbrook, Illinois: "When I was a kid my dad, and a few of the other dads, maybe four or five of them, helped out with out neighborhood team. We had a little park across the road from a tavern. They'd dump all the equipment and say, 'Okay, you boys get together and choose up teams and play.' Then they'd go across the street and have a couple of beers and let us play. Every hour or so my dad would stick his head out the door and walk to the edge of the road and rub his hand across his shirt a few times—you know, flashing me the hit and-run sign, or something. That's how we practiced. The kid who has the ability, the desire, if he plays it will surface. You can't force it."

Personally, I think Little League is valuable because it reminds us that the Parkers and the Winfields and the Reggie Jacksons are getting paid millions to play a game that small boys play for free. Which is one reason I find it hard to give kids advice, and so do most big-leaguers. The kids will learn soon enough that they have to find a style of their own.

For example, Pete Rose doesn't recommend his base-sliding technique, which is usually head-first, but he thinks it is a safer way to slide, on the theory that you are less likely to break your belly than your ankle or your leg. Also, you usually get your picture in the paper.

When someone asked Doug Rader what advice he would give a kid, he suggested that they eat bubble-gum cards. "Not the gum," he said, "but the cards. They have lots of good information on them."

Players are not always comfortable offering advice to youngsters, usually for reasons that are well-founded. Henry Aaron was asked once if he would like to teach the art of hitting to young players. "I'd like it very much," he replied, "but I wouldn't teach 'em to do it my way. I'd try to help a young player with his own style—not mine.

"I've got a hitch in my swing and I hit off the wrong foot. I've done it the wrong way my whole career."

Mike Marshall, who made his reputation as a relief pitcher who could work every day, urges kid pitchers not to experiment with trick pitches. What he won't do is tell them how HE did it. "On national television one season," he said, "I demonstrated how to throw a screwball. I specifically warned that no youngster under the age of fifteen should attempt to place his arm in this position because of possible injury.

"Immediately, I was deluged with letters from kids saying how they were working on their screwball and would I please tell them more." He wouldn't, and he didn't.

If there is one serious piece of advice I could give to kids, it would be this: *swing the bat*. Little League develops pitchers and discourages hitters. A ball is easier to throw than to hit at that age—at any age, actually. Nothing kills interest like failure. The kid who keeps striking out considers himself a failure, and he looks for something else to do.

Mike Marshall is right. A manager should not let his kid pitchers throw a screwball or a curve ball. Not only because of the risk to a young arm, but because such pitches take the fun out of the game for the kids who can't hit them.

I would tell a manager something else: No matter what the score, or the situation, let your hitters swing on a three-ball and no-strike count. Chances are he'll get a pitch he can handle, and if he does why shouldn't he swing? He's there to have fun. And a bat is no fun unless you swing it. Trust me.

In one respect, the Little Leagues achieved something that the big fellows never have: a really international World Series. An English writer, Brian Glanville, of London, once commented on this obvious American conceit: "It's very quaint. One team in the United States plays another team in the United States and is declared 'World' champion. We used to call the game 'rounders,' you know."

For years, the Little League World Series was regularly won by teams from Mexico, Taiwan, and Japan. There was a memorable scene in 1958, when a band of ragamuffins from Monterrey won the championship for the second year in a row.

The Mexican pitcher, a five-six beanpole named Hector Torres— who later made it to the majors as a shortstop—walked halfway to home plate as the final game came down to its last out. Mexico led, 10-1, over Kankakee, Illinois, with the bases empty and two away.

Torres doffed his cap and bowed low to his catcher, Carlos Trevino. *"Te dedico este bateador,"* he said. The hitter, not understanding Spanish, didn't know he had been insulted. Torres had said to his catcher: "I dedicate this batter to you."

It was a lovely gesture, and I am saddened to note that never in my entire career did a pitcher dedicate a hitter to me.

I owe a debt to Little-League baseball, and the debt should be acknowledged here and now. I was sitting by a pool with Merle Harmon in Anaheim, taking the rays, when Merle answered a call from Dennis Lewin, of ABC, in New York.

When Merle returned to his seat, he grinned and said ABC wanted me to fly to Williamsport, Pennsylvania, to telecast the Little League World Series with Keith Jackson.

I really didn't want to go. The Brewers had just arrived for a series against the Angels, and this was my first year (1973) of sharing the play-by-play with Harmon. I didn't feel in a position to be asking for favors. Also, working with a network, any network, was not one of my obsessions. I was not then, or now, a goal-oriented person.

Merle talked me into it. "You never know where it

might lead," he said. I flew across the country to Williamsport without even knowing what I would be paid—one thousand dollars, as it turned out. I did the Series with Keith and rejoined the Brewers.

A year later, ABC asked me to fly to New York to audition for the color spot on their Monday night baseball package, which would begin the next season. With Bob Prince, who was to do the play-by-play, I watched a silent videotape of a World Series game and recreated the action. They must have liked what they heard. I have been doing it ever since.

I guess that makes me another graduate of the Little Leagues.

PART V

Touching Some
Extra Bases

*In which he describes some of the great
players he admired, and some whose paths
he crossed, and some who were just his
kind of dustball. And a few stories straight
from the Hot Stove League.*

"The basic idea behind this book was to cover my
career and just talk about what a great guy I was. I
don't see how we can miss."

14. A Few of My Friends, and Then Some

WHEN A TEAM he was managing ended its season in winter ball, Doug Rader made a point of saying good-bye to one of his pitchers in the clubhouse. He told the fellow, a kind of nutcake, that he intended to request his services at Hawaii, where Rader would skipper San Diego's top farm club the next season.

The pitcher shook his head. "The way my arm feels right now," he said, frowning, "I don't even know if I'll be playing next season."

Rader jabbed him in the chest with a finger. "I don't care if you can throw or not," he said. "Every team needs a sick individual on it, and for me you're *it*."

Known in his playing days as the Red Rooster, Rader did not mean sick-sick, as in unhealthy. He meant goofy, off-the-wall, unpredictable, *weird*. It is a role Doug played on every team that employed him. As I did.

For the most part, Rader—the ex-Padre, ex-Astro, lifelong snowflake—was correct. But more and more today's teams are making an effort, a conscious one, I think, to get along without that kind of free spirit. The teams I see now, in my role as a broadcaster, can best be described as well-behaved, well-dressed young men building a base for that day when their arms or legs give out.

I can sum them up in two words: basically boring.

That remark is not a complaint, mind you, just a comparison. The teams of my day were less colorful than those of Babe Ruth's day, but the gap wasn't nearly as wide. We specialized in miscellaneous characters and that-was-burlesque humor. Hardly a flight took place that did not produce a scuffle, some tipsy barbershop harmony, or the occasional scream of a hostess darting up the aisle.

You never doubted the truth of the stories you heard, and an explanation was seldom required. No one ever explained what Turk Farrell was doing one night chasing Jim Owens through the halls of a Philadelphia hotel, both of them naked as newborn babes. They had been members of the famed Dalton Gang with the Phillies, later traded to Houston.

Farrell claimed that Owens had stabbed him with one of those desk pens you dip in an inkwell, and he had a blue dot on his bare hip to prove it.

In the 1960s, the cutting personal reference was as much a part of the game as hitting into a double play. A young catcher who had a low opinion of a veteran player's intellect didn't hesitate to let him know it: "Norm," he told him, "if it wasn't for baseball you'd be selling apples on a corner."

When a rookie infielder, a bonus baby, found himself in a terrible batting slump, an old hand advised him to switch to a lighter bat. The rookie said, yeah, with a lighter bat he could get around on the ball faster. The veteran said, "No, but it'll be easier to carry back to the dugout after you strike out."

I still hear that kind of affectionate cruelty in the bantering among the players of the 1980s. These players are smarter. I am not sure that they are better educated. And I would be reluctant to say that they love the game less than the players did when I broke in. But there is no doubt in my mind that they take themselves more seriously. Big money has that effect on people. It is like making out your will.

Today's players are more settled, more secure in their planning. Most of them have already picked out other careers. They have investments. They want to be seen and treated as responsible people. When the players board a plane, you see so many three-piece suits it looks like they have evacuated the offices of E. F. Hutton. You get the impression that management now picks a roster with the idea of getting the best possible team photograph.

When I was making around ten thousand dollars a year, you would begin to think about an off-season job in September. You thought in terms of unloading a beer truck.

Baseball has gone through such cycles before. The teams may go back to looking for players out of the Gashouse Gang, or the stick-it-in-his-ear school. Baseball people are great copycats. They will all try whatever wins for someone else. If one club finds a guy with hair all over his body and one eye in the middle of his forehead, and he eats glass and hits .400, soon you are going to see a lot of hairy, one-eyed glass-eaters around the league.

For now some of the fun is gone, and you don't have

to hunt long or far to understand why. When even the fringe players are knocking down a hundred grand a year, and more, you are not encouraged to cut up and take chances. In the past, it wasn't just the scrubs who horsed around, it was the stars, Mantle, Mays, Aaron, Spahn, who had the most laughs.

Of course, the conditions are not as favorable. You no longer have the wooden floors in the clubhouse, where you could nail a guy's shoes to the deck. Even the old bullpens are gone. Now they are all in the open, so the fans—and the manager—can see whatever is going on.

We used to run a closed society out there. Most of the people in the bullpen didn't care about starting. At least, we said we didn't. When a regular came down just to visit we chased him away. I mean, we protected our *turf*. It was like driving the snakes out of Ireland. Once, with the Phillies, Chris Short slipped down to the bullpen to hide from Gene Mauch before a game. He settled himself in a wheelbarrow and took a nap. While he slept, the rest of us tied him to the barrow, working like rodeo cowboys, using the ropes and chains the ground crew kept to drag the infield. When he woke up, and discovered he couldn't move, Chris yelled and cursed and carried on something fierce. We finally let him out fifteen minutes after the game had started.

A statement ought to be made about baseball humor. At its liveliest, it is crude and shameless and irreverent. It is army humor, with more sweat. For a few hours every day nothing exists outside the ball park. You are thrown together in this tight, remote, womanless (most of the time) world, and whether or not you like each other a bond is forged.

The team is everything. You are glad to belong, to be a

part of it, speeding along with it, or stumbling, as the case may be. Your body may be on a bus or a plane or in a hotel, but your mind is in the locker room, and the laughs grow out of this experience.

Two examples: In the early 1960s, a writer for *Sports Illustrated* heard that John Bateman, a catcher for the Houston Astros, was one of the funniest men in the big leagues. He followed the team for a week or two and kept asking for examples of Bateman's wit. The players assured him that the supply was endless, but nothing popped quickly to mind.

At last, one night behind the batting cage, an outfielder named Howie Goss approached the writer. "I've thought of a story that typifies Bateman's sense of humor," he said, "but I'm not sure you can use it."

"Don't worry about that," the man from *Sports Illustrated* said, whipping out his pad and pen. "I can fix the language."

Goss shrugged. "Well, one day X (the team's most popular player) was sitting on the crapper"—the writer's pen stopped in mid-stroke—"and Bateman called out, 'Hey, kid, did you weigh yourself before you got on there?'

"X said, no, why, and Bateman answered, 'In case you fall in, we want to know how much shit we have to fish out before we get to you.'"

The writer put his pad back in his hip pocket, gave a feeble laugh, and walked away.

A story out of Seattle a few years ago, when an expansion team was trying to survive there, captures some of the *esprit* of the bullpen. In the late innings of a losing game the bullpen was busy, as usual.

Ray Oyler, a reserve infielder, was warming up one of

the pitchers when he missed a sinker, and it caught him right on the cup. The pitch didn't bounce or tip his glove, it simply landed a direct hit. You hardly ever hear of that happening. The "twang" of ball striking metal echoed into the stands.

Oyler pitched forward, almost in slow motion, like a Tom-and-Jerry cartoon, and on all fours he started crawling toward the dugout, unable to cry out in pain or even make a sound. The players in the bullpen began to laugh, and the action came to a stop. He kept crawling. The laughter spread to the guys on the bench. Soon they were out of control. In the stands, the fans looked on, fascinated. Oyler reached the dugout, pulled himself onto a rail and threw up.

They were getting beat, and on the field people were running around the bases, and the Seattle players couldn't stop laughing. The manager, Joe Schultz, had to take off his glasses, wipe his eyes, and hide his head in the arm of his jacket.

The stadiums are bigger and fancier, the players higher paid and more secure, the fans less worshipful. But the baseball mentality hasn't changed in a hundred years.

Trust me. This is no mournful wail for a game that once was and will never be again. Memory can be a con man. Nostalgia should go back where it came from. The crackers in the ole cracker barrel were usually stale. Penny candy rotted your teeth just as fast when it didn't cost a quarter. Trains were dusty and bumpy and you were always getting a cinder in your eye.

As a product, baseball may be better than ever. I don't think so, but who knows? It is tempting to compare players, teams, and eras, and part of the fun is knowing that no one can prove us wrong. The arguments are forever. It is like judging pretty girls on a beach. The last one to walk by wins.

I am not sure when it dawned on me that the 1960s are the good old days to the young players of the 1980s. To this generation, Aaron, Allen, Mathews, Spahn, and Gibson, even Bo Belinsky, who lost more games than he won, are part of the mythology of the sport. I don't remember growing older. When did they?

It begins to sound like a singer or comic doing a Las Vegas lounge shtick when you say that, in the end, what lasts are the friendships you made. After you have blown the money and forgotten the batting averages and lost track of the wins and losses, the only thing that counts is the people.

Now I might not go quite that far. I knew some players whose friendship you would not have wished on J. R. Ewing, and who seemed to remember the exact count on every hit in their career. But I consider myself fortunate to have played on teams with men who, at what they did, were among the best, or the strangest, or the funniest who ever lived. I've touched on some of them earlier, but here they are again, a few of however many there were:

The Hammer

Henry Louis Aaron, as he is known in the *Baseball Register*, was the most underrated player of my time, and his. It may seem strange to make such a claim on behalf of the man who broke Babe Ruth's lifetime home run record, and went through the longest countdown the game has ever known.

But that's the point. Not until he collected his six hundredth homer in 1972, at the age of thirty-seven, did the press and fans catch on to what his opponents had always known: that Hank Aaron was one of a kind.

He had three things going against him: 1) He didn't play in New York or Los Angeles; 2) he was too predictable, meaning that most years he would get his forty homers, drive in a hundred runs and hit .320 . . . no surprises here; 3) he lacked showmanship. His cap didn't fly off when he caught a fly ball, and after a game you never saw him eat twenty hot dogs and wash them down with a six-pack of beer.

When Henry reached the majors in 1954, Ted Williams and Stan Musial were already legends. Willie Mays and Mickey Mantle were coming into their own. Aaron had been in the league eight or ten years— certainly it was after I had joined the Braves in 1962— before his name was mentioned with any of those. We would argue his case with out-of-town writers, and their eyes would glaze over.

I asked him once if he felt slighted. He said, "What difference does it make?"

I said, "You may not believe in beauty contests, but if you're in one you want the judges to vote you purty."

He shrugged.

I was a broadcaster with the Brewers, in 1976, when Aaron played out his string in Milwaukee, and hit the last of his 755 home runs. If you were to ask me what was the most remarkable thing about him, I would not single out any of the obvious points, his endurance, his power, his wrists. He had the quickest wrists I ever saw. Baseball scouts talked about Aaron's wrists the way male moviegoers of another time talked about Betty Grable's legs.

But none of it impressed me so much as how stable Henry has been. With the possible exception of Stan

Musial, it isn't likely that anyone played twenty years in the majors and changed less than Henry Aaron. For a fellow who came out of Southern poverty, who was one of the last players signed out of the Negro Leagues, and who met his share of prejudice on the way up, Henry seemed to have no rage in him.

One anecdote followed Aaron all through his career. The story revealed something about his nature. It also revealed how hard it was for the writers to come up with anecdotes about Henry.

During the 1957 World Series, the Yankee catcher, Yogi Berra, noticed that Aaron held the bat in a way contrary to the usual baseball practice. "Hey," said Berra, from his squat, "you got the bat facing the wrong way. Turn it around so you can see the trademark."

Henry continued to stare at the pitcher's mound. Out the side of his mouth, he said, "Didn't come up here to read. Came up here to hit."

Other players would marvel when they heard that Henry actually hit cross-handed when he signed with the Indianapolis Clowns. That is like playing a piano in handcuffs. In his first day in spring training, he began rifling base hits all over the park and the manager asked why he gripped the bat the way he did. Henry said it was the only way he knew.

Henry never confused chatter with conversation. He liked his privacy and his natural caution was sometimes taken for distrust.

Once he sat on a stool in front of his locker, an hour or so before game time, sorting two baskets filled with fan mail. His attention was diverted by a mild commotion at the clubhouse door.

"You can't come in here," an attendant was saying,

loudly, to a fellow who turned out to be Leroy Nieman, the sports artist.

"I just want to make a few sketches of Aaron," said Nieman, looking past the guard and catching the eye of Henry, who said nothing.

"We got a rule," said the attendant. "You can't come in here."

Nieman unzipped a leather case and began removing a sketchbook and other implements. "Okay," he said, agreeably, "then I'll just draw him right here, from the doorway." Twenty or thirty feet from his subject, he calmly sketched away.

Henry glanced up now and then as he disposed of the letters, flipping them into one basket or the other. Several minutes passed. Then the clubhouse man reappeared and motioned to the artist: "Hank says it's okay for you to come in."

Nieman pulled up a chair and without a word returned to his work. Aaron followed each stroke with interest. After a few minutes, he craned his neck to inspect the sketch. "You're not getting me," he said, with firmness. "You're not getting me."

"Take it easy," said Nieman. "You don't hit a homer every time up. I'm not finished."

More strokes. More color came alive on the sheet. "That's it," said Henry, his voice rising. "Now you got me. You got me."

When Nieman finished, Henry asked if he could have the sketch. "I don't give my work away," he was told.

Aaron looked startled. "People usually give me things like that," he said.

"I don't," said Nieman. "If you want mine you pay for it." He has a rack of black hair and a mustache that divides his face in half, and he is not intimidated by athletes. He grinned and added, "But I'll make a deal with you."

Nieman was in Atlanta to teach art classes to ghetto kids. He offered to trade the sketch if Aaron would pose for one of his classes. Henry agreed. You can guess how the kids reacted when their model turned out to be the home run king.

Henry did not talk much, even in the clubhouse, and what you learned about his early life came from stray remarks, spaced far apart. He was one of eight children, supported by a father who worked on the drydocks in Mobile. At eighteen, he joined the Indianapolis Clowns, where the meal money was two dollars a day. The players ate mostly out of grocery stores, on lunchmeat sandwiches.

He weighed 180 when he reached the big leagues, and he weighed the same when he retired. He was a small man as home run hitters go. He lacked the muscle or power of a Frank Robinson or a Frank Howard or a Willie Mays. He drove the ball with perfect wrists and perfect timing.

People used to say that the difference between Mays and Aaron was this: Willie attacked the game; Henry got it to cooperate. He was as smooth and effortless as a swan gliding along a lake.

Not many fans ever knew that the Giants could have had Mays and Aaron in the same outfield. Both the Giants and the Braves made bids after scouting him with the Clowns. Both wanted to start him in Class C, but the Braves offered him a Class A contract, worth two hundred dollars more a month. And for that difference, the Giants lost the man who would one day hit more home runs than Babe Ruth.

The Good-bye Kid

No player was more stubborn or more talented than Richie Allen, but he made up for it by being misunderstood.

Allen played for the Phillies, twice, the Cardinals, Dodgers, White Sox, and Oakland. Atlanta owned his contract at one time, but he never reported. He was described as a rebel, a militant, a truant, and a night walker. He was accused of having a drinking problem, an attitude problem and a keeping-track-of-time problem.

My kind of guy.

In truth, there was nothing wrong with Richie Allen's heart, or his instincts, but he felt a powerful resistance to having his mind made up for him. If he was pushed he tended to push back.

In baseball, this is the quickest way I know to be labeled a troublemaker. Once the label is attached it is hell to get off. Allen was the classic example of the guy who felt free only while he was playing the game. The rest of the time he wanted the world to go away. His clock started when the first pitch was thrown.

The Phillies signed Richie out of high school, at seventeen. He had the biceps of a heavyweight fighter and a thirty-inch waist and he could crush a baseball. He was just a kid, but so strong that people forgot to treat him like one—until he reached the majors. The wrong time and place.

I understood that part of him. We sat and talked and drank far into the night when we were teammates in Philadelphia, and he told me things I don't think he shared with many others.

His mother drove him to the airport, in Pittsburgh, when he caught the plane for his first trip to spring training. He was from the town of Wampum, in the same area of Pennsylvania that produced Joe Namath.

All the way to the airport, his mother gave Richie instructions on how to act. She had raised eight kids by doing day work and taking in laundry and sewing on the side. When you heard Richie talk about his mother, it was a hard image to square with all the headaches he had caused his managers.

"She kept telling me to remember my training at home," he said. "She told me to be sure and change my underwear every day. She told me to be careful what I ate. She also said she had packed a Bible and she handed me a slip of paper with instructions on what verses to read."

Richie had never been on a plane before. "I was scared stiff," he said. "The weather was rough. He knuckleballed all the way to Florida. Then when I got off in Clearwater I saw in the terminal that there were separate doors for white and colored. I had never seen this before and I was confused and frightened. If Bobby Del Greco (then a Philly player) hadn't come along and helped me, I probably would have gone back home."

He didn't join the team at its hotel in downtown Clearwater. He was taken to the home of a black woman and given a room. "After a while," he said, "they felt I might have been lonesome and they sent me company. It was Marcelino Lopez, a Cuban pitcher. We were great company for each other. He didn't speak English and I didn't speak Spanish."

In baseball, reputations are made or ruined in incidents that are small and sometimes silly. It isn't hard to pinpoint the exact moment that things started to go wrong for Allen. He was in his second season with the Phillies, and the team had landed at the airport in Los Angeles.

Frank Thomas, a veteran outfielder, large and a little klunky, flipped a quarter at Richie and said, "Hey, boy, take my bags!" He was only joking and meant no harm. But Allen was only twenty-two and not yet ready for that kind of humor.

That was the background for what happened a few days later at the batting cage in Philadelphia. Johnny Callison yelled across the cage to Thomas, calling him "Lurch," after a goonlike character on the television series *The Addams Family.* Thomas thought Allen had said it.

He yelled back, "There's no fence around me, Fifteen [Allen's number]. You may get a meal out of me, but I'll get a sandwich out of you."

Richie sprang at him. His punches came in a cluster, knocking Thomas down, and Frank responded by striking Richie on the shoulder with a bat. At that point the other players pulled them apart.

Later, in the clubhouse, Gene Mauch announced that anyone talking about the fight would be fined fifteen hundred dollars. Which explains why few of the details leaked out. Shortly, Thomas, whose gawky enthusiasm endeared him to the fans, was traded, and the boos began to swell for Richie Allen.

If ever a town had a love-hate relationship with a player, this was one in the making. They cheered his home runs and game-winning hits. But the boos deepened with each contract fight, each newspaper blast, each infraction.

The year after Richie injured his hand, with the papers and the fans thriving on the team's turmoil, Mauch moved to restore discipline. He ordered every player to be in his position on the field at 5:00 P.M., with no talking permitted. He had also appointed Allen as his captain.

Richie saw the move as an attempt to get him to accept responsibility. So he did. He went to Gene and told him that the players resented being treated like children. Recalls Richie: "He said that for every day I wasn't in position at five he would fine me a hundred and fifty dollars. It was a principle with me. I didn't show up—and I paid."

It became a team ritual, Allen arriving late or not at all for batting practice. The management was groping for an answer. The team knew it needed a happy, or at least an interested, Richie Allen to win. He was a threat to win the triple crown any year he was healthy. He was their big man. But only one man knew what went on inside his head, and Richie wasn't telling.

As a measure of his importance to the club, it is worth noting that on the night I was traded back to the Braves, in 1967, most of the concern in the clubhouse was for how Richie would react.

While I was driving in three runs with two doubles to give us a 9-8 win over the Cubs, in the second game of a doubleheader, the writers were being handed a press release. I was going to Atlanta for Gene Oliver.

As we trooped into the clubhouse, Gene Mauch motioned to a reporter, and said: "Tell those other guys not to tell anybody. Let them whoop it up a while before I call him in."

We stood around for ten minutes, shaking hands and snapping the tabs off cans of beer, before the word came that Mauch wanted to see me. In the *Daily News* the next afternoon, Bill Conlin wrote about Richie: "Allen was feeling desolate, even though he had just struck a homer that will become legend long after Connie Mack Stadium is torn down. Rich Allen is a man, but right then he felt like crying. You could see it in his eyes.

" 'I wish they were sending me instead,' he said softly. 'I wish they were sending us both. He was the best friend I've got on this club and now they're sending him away. That's the thing that bugs me about this game. You make a friend like him and then he's gone.' "

I know. Reading those words, you almost expect someone to lower his head and say, "Wherever he is, he'll be better off. He's at peace now."

Bo Geste

When I joined the Phillies in the spring of 1966, I knew Robert (Bo) Belinsky by reputation. *Everybody* knew Bo by reputation. You could not dislike him. He was a gassy guy, as Bo himself might put it, and probably did.

He was a man for all seasons: bon vivant, pool hustler, dog fancier, ladies' man and occasional left-handed pitcher.

It was often said of Belinsky, but never by Bo himself, that he had squandered his talent, had a great arm but not the discipline to use it and, finally, had thrown away his career for all the women he loved. Bo did not see things quite that way.

"I have never considered myself a great talent," I heard him say once. "I think I have gotten more publicity for doing less than any player who ever lived."

He may have been right. In his first five seasons in the majors, Bo won a total of twenty-five games and was traded three times. One way or another, he was seldom out of the headlines.

As a rookie with the Angels, he reported to Palm Springs a week late, called a press conference to explain that he had been delayed by a pool tournament, and then demanded a thousand-dollar raise.

That was for openers. In May he pitched a no-hitter against Baltimore and went on to win his first six games, all but standing baseball on its ear. There was not to be a flashier, more popular debut until Fernando Valenzuela came along in 1981.

Within a month Belinsky had bought a new Cadillac and acquired, more or less in order, a fiancée (Mamie Van Doren), a business agent, a lawyer and the readership of Walter Winchell. All on an annual salary of seven thousand dollars. He might have conquered the world.

"Instead," Bo said, "the no-hitter I pitched actually cost me money. I had to buy drinks for everyone. It was like making a hole-in-one."

In unrelated adventures, he once threw a blonde out of his car at five in the morning, slugged a sixty-four-year-old sportswriter, married a former Playmate of the Year, and adopted a stray, part-cocker spaniel named Alfie.

The dog became the mascot of the Houston club and was given its own sandbox in the clubhouse. The players accepted Alfie as easily as they accepted Bo, although Barry Latman, a pitcher, asked wearily, "How am I going to explain to my wife that I got a locker next to a dog?"

For a while they were inseparable. His teammates joked that you could always tell them apart because Alfie was the one who was serious about baseball.

If much of Bo's career was a con, it was a harmless con that did injury to no one but Bo. Wherever he went he may not have won a lot of games, but he was good for the club because he kept the manager and the writers busy.

Bo was street-smart. To engage him in conversation was like catching Bernard Baruch on his park bench or Snoopy on his doghouse. He is the author of such philosophical gems as: "Happiness is a first-class pad, good wheels, an understanding manager and a little action."

He had a fine eye for caricature. It was Bo who pointed out that Philadelphia fans "would boo a funeral." Hawaii "is where the goodies are." And when Houston threatened to ship him to its top farm club, he shrugged: "Oklahoma City is nice, if you bring enough Alka-Seltzer."

The few times I caught Bo, he still had the lively arm and enough stuff to win. What he didn't have was the frame of mind, the intensity you found in a Spahn, a Gibson, or a Koufax. He enjoyed the cheers, but didn't need them as a steady diet.

Whether Bo was overrated in the romance league, I can't say, but I saw him in action and can assure you that he did not believe his own publicity. "If I did everything they said I did," he confided, "I'd be in a jar at the Harvard Medical School."

In Los Angeles, Bo was often in the company of such beautiful women as Mamie, Ann-Margret and Tina Louise, when he was not in the company of Walter Winchell, the famed gossip columnist who had taken him under his wing.

That era is gone forever. The line between sports and the arts has been so blurred that the two sides are no longer so enthralled with each other. Babe Ruth once made the Broadway scene, and Hollywood swept up Bo, but it doesn't happen that way anymore.

Bo still had the telegram Winchell sent him, after he had been quoted on a road trip as saying that he knew his Hollywood friends would drop him if he stopped winning. Winchell printed the wire in his syndicated column and possibly sent copies to Mr. and Mrs. America and all the ships at sea:

"DEAR BO:

"YOU DON'T KNOW ME VERY WELL YET, KID. I'M THE GUY WHO PREFERS TO BE WITH LOSERS. I'M THE GUY WHO WROTE 'THERE IS NOTHING AS LONELY AS A LOSER'S DRESSING ROOM.' I WOULD LIKE IT VERY MUCH IF YOU NEVER WON ANOTHER GAME SO I COULD CONVINCE YOU OF THAT.

"A CHAMPION IS ONE WHO GETS UP FOR ONE MORE ROUND. IF THEY EVER KICK YOU OUT OF BASEBALL FOR BEING A BAD BOY YOU WILL FIND OUT THAT I PRACTICE WHAT I PREACH: TO WIT, A REAL FRIEND IS ONE WHO WALKS IN WHEN THE REST OF THE WORLD WALKS OUT. SIGNED. WALTER WINCHELL."

It was beautiful. It was also just about the last word Bo heard from Winchell as he began his descent to the minors, the Phillies, Houston, the minors, the Cardinals, the minors, the White Sox, and out of baseball.

I doubt that he left the game with any serious regrets. Baseball was never his passion, it just paid his motel bill.

If he made no other lasting contribution to the sport, Bo destroyed most of the universal theories about sex and baseball.

As Bo remembered it, managers were always telling him not to engage in indoor recreation on nights before he pitched. They recommended that he rest and save himself for after the game. But Belinsky had a problem. He had no interest after the game. Neither the spirit nor the flesh was willing.

Besides, he had rejected the night-before theory after his no-hitter with the Angels. He was still looking for the girl who had left his bed that morning. "This was some kind of good-luck girl," he recalled, his dark eyes glowing. "But she disappeared from the picture. I'd met her at a steak house. Here I was with an ordinary secretary, probably—no flashy gal in any way, but a very lean, beautiful gal. And this was how I trained for my no-hitter, and it came in."

Bo never found her, proof of which is that he never had another winning season.

Horseman, Pass This Way

I am reminded of Inspector Clouseau, the Peter Sellers character, who was always being ambushed by his valet, Kato.

In St. Louis, I had a roommate like Kato, except he was taller and balder and less Oriental-looking. For a guy who later went straight, and became a big-league manager, Roger Craig had as much deviltry in him as the worst of us. His sense of humor ran to Halloween pranks.

No matter where we were, or what we were doing, Roger had this compulsion to scare people. He would turn over trash cans as you walked down the street, or thump the side of the car as you drove. God forbid you should have to get up at three in the morning to use the toilet. When you eased out of the bathroom, he would be pressed against the wall, on the other side of the door, ready to let out a bloodcurdling scream. Or he might throw a wastebasket across the room.

Even when you knew it was coming, and braced yourself, the experience was still hard on the nerves. At such times I would ask myself if this was any kind of life for a grown person.

But it was easy to forgive Craig his occasional looniness. He was bright, he had guts, he could pitch and he had once lost twenty games for the New York Mets, sixteen of them in a row, and you were inclined to give him a little benefit of the doubt. I mean, he had suffered for his art.

Craig came over from the Mets in the middle of the 1964 season, pitched well out of the bullpen as the Cards drove to the pennant, and then won the fourth game of the World Series against the Yankees in relief.

Craig's looks were deceptive. He was tall and gangly, with a long, sad, gentle face. But he was physically tough, an outdoorsman, and good company if you didn't let him sneak up on you.

On our first road trip to Los Angeles, Roger invited me to stay at his home. He owned a riding stable nearby, and the next morning he insisted that we go horseback riding. Naturally, I had no proper clothes with me, so Roger loaned me a shirt and a pair of his Levi's. Craig is six-six. I'm six-one. When we walked up to the stables I must have looked like Emmett Kelly. I caught the stable hands exchanging looks. They were thinking, "Get a load of this Elwood."

Roger picked out one of his daughter's horses for me and we started down a trail, which was actually a flood-control ditch. We found ourselves at a parking lot on one of the main streets, and we tied the horses to some cars and walked into a restaurant to have lunch.

Craig sauntered inside like he was the sheriff of Dodge City. Everyone else was wearing suits and ties and we were in Levi's with horseshit on our shoes. I never did get my wingtips clean.

We ordered a sandwich and a couple beers, then headed home. On the way back, Roger began to tell me what a great trick horse he was riding, how he could get off and the horse was trained to follow him.

With that he said, "Watch this, Uke," and he swung his leg over the back of the horse and dropped to the ground. Thirty seconds later, the horse bolted away and headed for home, his hooves kicking up small clouds of dust as the distance between us widened.

Roger did a double take and said, "Jeezus, Uke, quick, get off your horse so I can go catch him."

I said, "Your ass. Go catch him yourself. If I get off this horse I know what will happen to me."

He walked alongside us for the next two miles, bitching every step of the way.

Little Big Man

I learned a long time ago never to get into a fight with a person who comes up to your waist. You never know where their punches will land, and God forbid they should bite.

No one has ever accused Donald Davidson of not fighting fair, not in a forty-five-year career that has made him one of the most distinctive figures in baseball. No one in the sport has a bigger heart, not a player or manager—need I include umpires and owners?—and that is a lot to say for someone who stands four feet, two inches high.

With his feisty nature, Donald stands out in a crowd, especially if the crowd is on its hands and knees. In such a case he would probably pass out his business card, which is one inch by two inches and resembles a large postage stamp.

It is safe to say that among National-League players, and among the fans of Milwaukee and Atlanta, no front-office type is as well known, or as popular, as Donald.

One afternoon he strolled through the streets of downtown Milwaukee with John Quinn, the general manager of the Braves. Every few feet a friend, or a fan, would stop Donald and greet him. Quinn looked on with growing amusement, then asked one stranger, "Tell me, how did you recognize Donald in his dark glasses?"

For forty years, Davidson gave his all to the Braves, first as a clubhouse boy, in the days when Lefty Grove was their star pitcher and the team traveled by train. Then he moved up to publicist, assistant to the president, and traveling secretary. His odyssey with the team took him from Boston to Milwaukee to Atlanta. He was their link to the past. Hall of Famers, managers, owners, entire cities had come and gone. But Donald went with the franchise, like the Indian head on the team uniform.

Then the unthinkable happened. In April of 1976, Donald was fired by Ted Turner, the team's new owner, who suffered what he himself later admitted was a colossal mental lapse. It was as if someone had bought the original thirteen American colonies and fired the American eagle.

As traveling secretary for the Braves, responsible for the team's housing, Donald always occupied a suite where he served as host to the press and other dignitaries. I guess what offended Ted was the fact that Donald could have slept in a bureau drawer, much less a suite.

But word of Donald's luxury reached Turner in a bad mood. The Braves were in a losing streak, as they often are. He decided that if standard rooms were good enough for the players, they ought to be good enough for Donald. Quite possibly, Turner didn't know that the Braves weren't paying for those suites. They are tossed in by hotels, grateful for the team's business.

Even if Atlanta had been paying, you had to wonder how Turner could hand out millions to players like Andy Messersmith and Claudell Washington, and try to reduce the living standards of a class act like Donald Davidson.

One word led to another, as they usually do, and the Braves and Donald parted company, after four decades. The next time Turner saw the little man, he had been hired for the same duties at more money by the Houston Astros, and the wrath of the public had alerted Ted to the size of his error.

"I guess I was wrong, Donald," he apologized. "Even my little boy gave me hell when he heard about it."

"It's okay," said Davidson. "You did me a favor."

The firing of a publicist, a traveling secretary, or even a general manager doesn't usually attract much attention. But Donald was different. Opinion was solidly against Turner, a famous yachtsman who has won the America's Cup and other great prizes.

But the general reaction was that Turner was probably accustomed to tight quarters. He might even sleep in a hammock. But he was in no position to compare himself with Davidson. How many Hall of Famers has ever dropped by his room for refreshments?

Had he ever been detained by Scotland Yard for looking at Buckingham Palace through binoculars from his hotel? When Donald did this in London, the British suspected that some alien ring working with an elf was trying to get information on the queen's movements.

All of which means that today Donald Davidson is smaller than life, if not more so. He is famous for his temper, his tireless spirit, and for winding up as the ironic victim of frequent jokes. One of the legends of baseball is the night he stepped into a hotel elevator with Warren Spahn and Lew Burdette.

He looked up from his key. "Punch twenty-six," said Donald, who couldn't reach that high.

Spahn exchanged cagey glances with Burdette. "We're only going to twenty-four," he said.

"Punch twenty-six, you s.o.b.," screamed Donald.

The two pitchers tumbled out of the elevator at the twenty-fourth floor, laughing, leaving Davidson to descend to the lobby. There he summoned the clerk and roared: "How many times have I told you never to give me a room above the third floor?"

In spirit and stature, if not in bloodline, Donald is related to Pearl Du Monville and Eddie Gaedel.

Created by the typewriter of James Thurber, Du Monville was a midget who became a part of baseball's library by pinch-hitting in a big-league game. The game took place in the pages of a short story entitled, "You Could Look It Up."

Thurber had a grand idea but no franchise. It was left to Bill Veeck to turn fiction into fact, for in 1953 Veeck sent Eddie Gaedel—thirty-six inches tall—to bat for the St. Louis Browns against the Detroit Tigers. Gaedel walked. The nation's sports pages the next day showed this wonderful picture of Bob Swift, the Detroit catcher, on his knees trying to provide a target for his pitcher.

Donald never swung a bat for the Braves, but it wasn't because he didn't want to strike a blow for his team. One way or another, he did.

One year, when the Braves were playing the Dodgers in a spring game at Sarasota, he was set up by the general manager of the Dodgers. Buzzy Bavasi told an elderly gatekeeper that a midget from the Ringling Brothers Circus would attempt to sneak into the park. "He'll get pretty nasty when you turn him down, and he'll make lots of threats," he cautioned. "But keep him out, and use force if necessary."

Then Bavasi hid in a passageway and watched as Donald appeared, loaded with record books and fact sheets and a brisk manner. In the argument that followed, the old fellow punched him in the nose.

The blow sent Donald sprawling. He picked up his sunglasses, gathered up his papers and then darted between the gatekeeper's legs and into the park. "You dirty bastard," he shouted over his shoulder.

When Birdie Tebbetts, then the vice-president of the Braves, and their former manager, heard that Donald had been slugged he went off to defend his honor. "Who did it?" Birdie demanded. "Nobody punches one of my men and gets away with it."

So Tebbetts was directed to the press gate. He looked at the gatekeeper, judged him to be around eighty years old, and turned around without a word.

When he encountered Donald, he said, "Thanks for getting hit by an old guy. You probably saved me from a beating."

This kind of craziness was common among clubs in

those years, and could go back and forth until the original complaint was forgotten.

Donald nursed his sore nose for several days, and his grudge for quite a bit longer. But that spring he got even with Bavasi. When the Dodgers showed up at Milwaukee's camp for a game, Buzzy walked up to the press entrance and identified himself.

"I'm sorry, sir," he was told, "but I have orders not to let you in without a pass from Mr. Davidson."

Of course, Donald needed no outside agitators as long as Spahn and Burdette were around. Once, after the players and officials had posed for a team picture, Spahn and Burdette threw him down and removed his trousers.

Donald bided his time. The next time Spahn went out to pitch, he strolled into the clubhouse, gathered up every garment he saw, including Spahn's socks, and tosed them into the shower, with the water running.

They say that when Spahn left the park that night, after he had dried his clothes as best he could, he looked like Ichabod Crane.

Clete Boyer and I once bought Donald a motor scooter, what kids call a mini-bike, for Christmas. We planned to deliver it on the appropriate day, but on Christmas Eve we sat around drinking in Clete's apartment and decided not to wait.

Our plan was to leave the scooter on his doorstep, ring the bell and hide in the bushes as he discovered his gift. Instead, we peeked into the house and saw Donald walking around. Clete checked the front door, found it unlocked and left it open. I drove the scooter right into the vestibule of the house.

His two dogs circled me, barking and snarling, followed by Donald, barking and snarling. Followed by several guests we didn't know he was entertaining. After a couple drinks, Donald settled down and we left.

The next morning, on his initial ride, he crashed the scooter into a mailbox and broke two ribs. The next time we saw Donald on the machine, it had training wheels. And that was how he kept it, when he rode around the field at spring training every year, wearing a motorcycle helmet Boyer and I had given him.

Donald is the object of endless one-liners. The players say his suits are made by Mattel. He isn't defensive about his size, the result of a siege of sleeping sickness when he was six.

He gets into situations that are not of his own making, but he grins and bears them. He was the unwitting cause, for example, of an engineering problem at Candlestick Park in San Francisco.

When the stadium was completed, it featured a fine, roomy, glass-enclosed press box. There was just one thing wrong with it. The work shelf was so high, and the seats so low, you couldn't see home plate. This loss tends to interfere with one's enjoyment of a baseball game, and the working press complained long and bitterly.

After many complaints and phone calls, a city architect came out to see what could be done to correct the problem. His visit coincided, unfortunately, with the arrival of the Braves for a series.

The architect walked in, discovered Donald Davidson sitting at a typewriter, perched on two pillows, and stormed out, convinced that the entire protest was a practical joke.

It was years before they ever raised the seats in the press box at Candlestick Park.

The Big D

In a tight spot, Don Drysdale looked at a batter digging in at the plate the way he would look at a snake crawling through the kitchen door.

Not many hitters dug in against him. He was an artist whose work I enjoyed watching. He is another one whose name is called when you talk about pitchers who were mean and tough.

I used to admire Drysdale's theory about the brush-back or knockdown pitch—a part of every pitcher's basic weaponry. He would place the first one under your chin and put you on your pants. It was what Branch Rickey called a "purpose" pitch. It was meant to plant a thought, a fear. Then, when the hitter got up, dusted himself off and took his stance, the second pitch was the one that did the job.

There was a night when Drysdale was pitching for the Dodgers against the Phillies and Robin Roberts. As the night wore on, several Phillies were forced to dive into the nearest foxhole to avoid being hit by pitches. Not all of them dived in time. Gene Mauch took the target practice as a personal affront, and he ordered Roberts to retaliate when Drysdale came to bat. He wanted Drysdale to get plugged. Roberts declined. He was the kind of guy who wouldn't hurt a fly.

So Mauch looked for someone who would, and he turned to Turk Farrell, who lumbered out to the mound. His first pitch to Drysdale sailed three feet over his head. Mauch perched himelf on the top steps of the dugout, cupped his hands and yelled: "I said KNOCK HIM DOWN!"

This time the tall Dodger righthander went sprawling. As he dusted himself off, he was getting red around the ears. Don is a nice-looking guy, well groomed, and he doesn't like dirt any better than the next fellow.

So Drysdale teed off on the two-and-oh pitch and doubled to the wall. As he pulled up at second base, he yelled out to the mound: "There's your knockdown pitch, Farrell."

At that Turk turned and fired to second, trying to pick off the runner, it says here. The throw was hard and straight and caught Drysdale on the hip. "There's your two-base hit, Drysdale," he said.

As luck would have it, I heard the story from both parties over the years, and in all the important details there is no disagreement. Both, in fact, seemed rather fond of the episode, and its aftermath.

It came to pass that during the winter the Phillies traded Farrell to the Dodgers, of all teams, and the first thing he did in spring training was look up Drysdale and make his peace. Turk was six feet four and could hold his own in a bar fight. But Drysdale stood six-six and had a memory at least that long.

"Well, Don, old buddy," said the Turk, with a hearty grin, "we're teammates now. Whaddaya say? Let bygones be bygones."

"Okay," said Drysdale, shaking his hand. "And it's a good thing. I had your name in my book." He meant it, too. Drysdale pulled out a notebook, and turned to a page with a list of names on it, and there at the top was Farrell's.

There is no question in my mind that Drysdale's record of fifty-eight and two-thirds scoreless innings—six straight shutout games—was the darndest thing ever achieved by a guy who throws a ball. It is a record I doubt will ever be broken. Today it is a rarity for a pitcher to even finish six straight games, much less do it without allowing a run.

Drysdale was one of the people you would pay to watch pitch, and good enough at bat that the Dodgers sometimes used him as a pinch hitter. I liked his style even when we were on different teams, and I liked him more after we got to know each other through our work at ABC.

Don told me once that when I turned up in the Braves' lineup on a night in 1967, his manager, Walter Alston, asked him how he planned to pitch to me. He said, "Damned if I know, I've never seen him play." He was probably right. I had been in the league six years, and so seldom started against a righthander that I had never faced him.

That night I went three-for-four and walked once, one of my hits a bullet that went right between his legs. Don said he knew then that he was nearing the end of the line. He retired two seasons later.

A Dry Gibson

I caught a few great pitchers and batted against several others, although they may not have been as great as I sometimes made them appear.

But if I had to pick one pitcher, to start one game that my team simply dare not lose, Bob Gibson would be near the top of the list. If he was not in a class by himself, it did not take long to call the roll: Spahn, Koufax, Drysdale . . . take your choice. I would take him for the same reason Johnny Keane gave when he called on Gibson on two days' rest to pitch the seventh game of the 1967 World Series: "I had a commitment to his heart."

Gibson was one of the best athletes I ever saw. He had been a baseball and basketball star at Creighton, and he was another, like Aaron and Allen, whose story was familiar: up from poor. His father died three months before he was born. His mother worked in a laundry. He remembered the first home he ever lived in, a four-room shack on Omaha's north side, as the place where a rat bit him on the ear.

I don't think the man ever lived who hated to lose more than Bob Gibson. He was a quick learner who, if you gave him a week, could beat you at your own game.

However, the first time he ever let himself get talked into a celebrity golf tournament, he shot a score of 115. It was his own fault. He counted all his strokes.

In the privacy of the clubhouse, he was known as a practical joker, a fellow who would sing, strum a guitar or join in whatever was going on. But others saw him as a guy wound tight, cold to strangers and uneasy in crowds.

I used to study Gibby. He was one of those rare individuals who seemed to be driven best by anger. Different pitchers reacted in different ways. Before a big game, dry wit rolled off the tongue of a Whitey Ford. Sandy Koufax was quiet and unfailingly polite. A Ray Sadecki would go around looking for conversation, and a Denny McLain would be on the phone to his booking agent, lining up dates to play the accordion.

But Gibson did it his own way. He would be aloof, haughty, or snappish, building up a determination that was something to behold. Winning is important to every professional athlete. With Gibson the urge was overpowering. His makeup demanded it. He primed himself mentally for the big games, but if you asked him how, he could only shrug and say, "No special way. It's just in me."

On the field he was a lion, who twice came back from broken legs and in the final week of the 1964 pennant race started or relieved in four out of six games.

Unlike Allen, who liked people but whose actions confused them, or Aaron, who went about his job like a guy building a pyramid, Gibson had an electric presence, but was never comfortable with fame. He was abrupt with writers and uncertain with fans. When one asked for his autograph in a restaurant in Detroit, Bob said, sure, as soon as he finished his dinner. The guy tore up his sheet of paper and threw it on the table. Another time a little old lady grew angry and made a scene because Gibby wouldn't join her and her guests. And a small boy, in his eagerness to obtain the valuable Gibson signature, poked him in the eye with a pencil.

I heard him say often that he did not believe in hero worship and lacked the right disposition for either end of it. What he had was the perfect disposition for a righthanded pitcher.

In his middle years he developed a hard curve to go with his slider and fastball. But his money pitch was always the fast one, which sometimes rose and sometimes sank. You never knew which was coming.

I caught Gibson on a night when he struck out thirteen in Milwaukee, my home town, and he never had better stuff. It was a big moment for me, playing in front of my friends and relatives, handling one of the game's fastest pitchers.

With two out in one of the late innings, and two strikes on the hitter, he cut loose with a pitch that moved so sharply I didn't have time to raise my glove, and it smacked against my bare hand. It felt as if I had put my palm flat against a hot stove. I picked up the ball with my mitt, tagged the runner, walked away from the plate, walked into the dugout and up the runway toward the clubhouse, and then cut loose with a scream that would have Johnny Weissmuller sound like a sissy.

Gibson came looking for me. He knew what I was doing, that I didn't want to carry on in front of my hometown folks. He grinned, and nodded, and went back to the dugout. It hurt, but it was what we called in baseball a good hurt.

Leave Us Eddie Mattress

When Eddie Mattress was seventeen, it was a very good year (1949). He had all his hair and the kind of apple cheeks that old ladies and young girls like to pinch. He didn't own a car. He lived on the third floor of a boarding house four blocks from the ball park, and he walked it both ways.

What he did own was a batting average of .363 for his first summer in the baseball boondocks, down in North Carolina. The future beckoned clear and strong. Eddie would chase it to the Hall of Fame, and the most prolific home run career any third baseman ever knew. Wherever he went, glory and groceries followed him. The trail led to Atlanta and Milwaukee in the minors, and when he returned to those cities years later he brought the big leagues with him.

He is the only player I know who can make such a claim.

He was not yet twenty-one when he joined the Braves, still in Boston, an old and faded club trying to rebuild.

Among the rookies they brought in were Mathews, and a shortstop named Johnny Logan, and a young pitcher obtained from the Yankees, Lew Burdette.

That winter the team chartered a plane. They painted the sides with the name "The Rookie Rocket," piled aboard a dozen Boston writers and flew across the country to interview a dozen of their hottest prospects, the ones who would restore the Braves to greatness.

But not in Boston.

"The Rookie Rocket," Eddie would laugh about it years later, "never got off the ground. We finished last that season . . . way, way back. We were either very old or very young. We had graybeards like Earl Torgeson and Walker Cooper on the club. And kids like myself and Logan.

"We were so bad that we used to pray for rain. No kidding. The day the season ended, the manager, Cholly Grimm, let all the extra players go home early. On the bus after the game we had more writers than players.

"I hit a double in the top of the ninth to tie the game, and when I got back to the dugout everybody was mad as hell. They wanted to get home. We were playing the Dodgers, and they had already locked up the pennant, and the game didn't mean anything.

"After twelve innings the score was still tied, and the umpires called it on account of darkness. The sun was still out."

I always liked to hang around with Eddie, not only because he had a special corner in the history of the Braves. He was just a helluva guy and the biggest spender the club ever had. Nobody ever picked up a check around him. He bought drinks and dinner for everyone.

I roomed with Eddie on the road except when the team

was in Los Angeles, where he stayed with his mother. Then Bob Buhl and I moved into the suite the Braves provided for Mathews. There was always a refrigerator filled with beer.

After a game one night at Dodger Stadium, Buhl and I sat down and started popping beer tabs and telling baseball stories. The nostalgia was flowing nearly as fast as the beer, when I noted the room had a fireplace.

I said, "Why don't we start a fire and make it just like home?"

Buhl said, "Yeah, why not?" We had the air conditioner going and were feeling kind of laid back.

I threw a bunch of newspapers into the fireplace, and the cardboard from the six-packs we had already polished off. When the fire got going fairly well, I tossed in four bats that Mathews kept in the room for practice. He would swing them constantly. The bats didn't really burn that well because the fire wasn't hot enough, but for about ten minutes Buhl and I were in heaven. It was then that the sprinkler system went off. The floor we were on began to fill with smoke, and we discovered that it was a false fireplace. Shortly, the hotel manager appeared, accompanied by Donald Davidson, who took care of the problem, one way or another.

Mathews came back to the room the next morning. I had stacked his bats next to the fireplace, all blackened and smokey, but otherwise unharmed. Eddie went into a rage, but he gave up when Buhl and I couldn't stop laughing.

As a Milwaukee kid, I knew how large a role Mathews had played in what became known as The Milwaukee Story. The Braves drew two million fans in Wisconsin after they left Boston, and their success in Middle America inspired Walter O'Malley to move the Dodgers to Los Angeles, and Horace Stoneham's Giants tagged along to San Francisco, launching the expansion boom in all of professional sports.

In those years Mathews was the symbol of the Braves, the only survivor of the team that arrived from Boston, on its way to Atlanta.

On opening day of 1965, in what would be the team's last season in Milwaukee, a local group brought back most of the Braves who had played in County Stadium in 1953.

One by one the players were introduced, waving their caps and trotting out to their old positions, standing alongside the player who was the current keeper of it. When the ceremonies ended, only one player stood alone, at third base, the only player who had been a Brave in 1953 who was still with the club. And out in the bleachers a group of fans unfurled a banner that must have been sixty feet wide. It read: "ATLANTA YOU CAN HAVE THE REST . . . LEAVE US EDDIE MATTRESS, OUR HERO."

Mattress was as close as some of the old German burghers of Milwaukee could come to pronouncing his name. When he saw the banner Eddie swallowed hard, tipped his cap and looked down at his shoes as though he had never seen them before.

Of all the records he achieved in the years he spent in the home of the Braves, wherever that happened to be, Mathews cherished most the one he set with Henry Aaron: most home runs in a career by teammates (863). They broke a record previously held by a couple of fellows named Babe Ruth and Lou Gehrig.

"I'm not a crusader about race or creed," Eddie told the press, "but I think the fact that Hank is colored and

I'm white, and we set this record together, well, I think that is kind of significant."

A Long and Twisty Road

Satchel Paige was sixty-two years old, wore bifocals, and looked almost grandfatherly when the Atlanta Braves signed him as a pitcher-coach in 1968. It was an act of grace by the team's owner, Bill Bartholomay, to qualify the old fellow for his pension.

That was the only time our paths crossed, but every ballplayer was curious about the gangly patriarch who may have been the greatest pitcher who ever lived.

One day Dizzy Dean visited the ball park. Henry Aaron asked Dean if Paige could *really* throw, asking the question mainly for Satch's benefit, just to hear how Dean would react.

"Could he throw?" repeated Dizzy. "Is a pig pork? You bet he could throw. Listen. He was quick. Me and him would pitch in exhibitions and it sounded like firecrackers going off. Warming up it was like double-barreled shotguns. Boom-boom! That's all you'd hear. Cotton came out of the mitts. We'd saw the bats off . . . right at the top."

The Braves put Paige on their roster just long enough (158 days) to give him the time he needed for his pension. He never got into a game, although Lord knows he thought he could still pitch. He described his repertoire of pitches as the blooper, looper and drooper, the jump ball, hurry ball and nothing ball, and the ever-dangerous bat dodger. It disturbed him to see today's young pitchers use only their arms and not their heads. "They throw the two-strike pitch over the plate," he complained one day. "They don't waste it. Me, on a two-strike pitch, they get something from me a dog wouldn't want to hit."

Satchel spent his time that summer singing of the old days, spreading good will and jiving the troops. He was living at the Dinkler Plaza Hotel in Atlanta.

One day I got on the pay phone in the clubhouse, rang the switchboard upstairs and had them put me through to the house phone a few feet away. I asked for Satchel Paige. When he picked up the phone, I put on my best German accent and told him I was the manager of the hotel.

I said, "I vant you to get your schidt oudt of your room, ve got a chentz to rent your room."

Satchel said, "Hey, who the hell you say this is?"

I gave him a name, Hans Gruber.

He said, "Gruber, what the hell you tawkin' about? I pay my rent by the month and my rent is paid."

I said, "Look, I don't give a schidt vat you pay or who you tink you are. To me you just a wrinkled old man, and the Braves haf gone downhill effer zintz you came. So you get your schidt out of the room."

We were talking on the phone ten feet apart and the conversation ended with Satchel announcing that he was on his way to the hotel to kick my ass.

I let him hang up the phone, watched him go over to his locker and start taking his uniform off. He only dressed to pitch batting practice, so I let him get halfway undressed before I let him in on the gag. He didn't mind. Clubhouse humor, the endless pranks, delighted him.

The Phillies had Satchel in 1958 on their farm club at Miami with kids like Dick Farrell, Don Cardwell, Ed Bouchee and others destined for the majors. Farrell remembered how the younger cult tormented Satch by putting dead fish in his shoes and nailing his uniform to the ceiling. But Satch always had the last laugh.

"He would warm up by putting a silver chewing-gum wrapper on the plate and pitching for it," said Farrell. "In Columbus, Ohio, there was a knothole in the outfield fence. A hitter got five thousand dollars for a home run through it. Of course, nobody ever collected. Satch said he could hit the hole from twenty feet. The guys laughed. He missed it five times. Then the betting started and Satch hit it three times in a row."

No one knows what feats Paige might have performed in the twenty years he was barred from the majors because of the color of his skin. He was a star in both leagues, the black one and the white one. Dean and Bob Feller both called him the greatest pitcher they ever saw. In his prime, Satch slept on his suitcase in Southern towns, barnstorming for one hundred dollars a game. In 1934 he beat Dean four out of six on one tour, when Dean was a thirty-game winner in the big leagues and a World Series hero.

When Satchel gained his first fame in the Negro Leagues in 1926, Joe DiMaggio was eleven years old. By 1935 Satchel had become a legend, and DiMaggio was still a year away from his rookie season with the Yankees.

When Bill Veeck brought Satch to the majors at Cleveland in 1948, Joe was baseball's greatest star. In 1952, by then with the Browns and back with Veeck, Paige was voted the American League's best relief pitcher. DiMaggio had been retired for two seasons.

Veeck gave him his first, overdue break not only in the interest of justice. He wanted to reinforce a weak Cleveland bullpen, and the move won the pennant for the Indians. To some it smacked of a publicity stunt.

In the *Sporting News*, J. G. Taylor Spink editorialized: "Many well wishers of baseball fail to see eye to eye with the signing of Satchel Paige, the superannuated Negro pitcher. To bring in a pitching rookie of Paige's age is to demean the standards of baseball in the big circuits."

Years later, Satchel noted: "I demeaned the big circuits considerable that year. I won six and lost one."

In the office of the baseball commissioner, the birth date of Paige is listed as July 7, 1906. Chances are that not even Satch knows for certain his actual age. What he does say, with the purest of logic, is: "It must have been meant for me to be bawn when I was . . . or I wouldn't have been bawn. If there hadn't been a color line, I might have made more money and got into trouble with Sam. This way, the whole world got to see me pitch."

His every move was one of melancholy. He could Bogart a cigarette with the best of them, holding it between his thumb and index finger. His eyes were slow and sad, his face long and wrinkled. "We seen some sights, it and I," he once said, fondly, observing his face in a mirror.

It seems strange to me even now to realize that segregation was still practiced in the South when I went to my first big-league training camp, not that long ago, in 1961. The black players lived apart from the team in Florida. They were not housed in the same motels or served in the same cafés as the whites.

They stayed in rooming houses and ate their meals with families that boarded them. In Bradenton, they stayed at Mrs. Gibson's. She served the best fried chicken in town, and we made jokes about it: how they ate better than the white guys, home-cooked meals and no curfew or bed checks.

At least, we have a way of marking where we have been. And how far we have to go. It isn't generally known, but Jackie Robinson not only broke the color line, he got the blacks into the dining rooms. Even when all the players began sleeping in the same hotels—I mean in cities like St. Louis, not some pit stop in the South—it was still standard practice for the blacks to order room service, so as not to offend whites in the dining room.

One night in Cincinnati, Jackie Robinson decided to enter the dining room and ask for a table. The captain seated him, the waiter served him, and none of the diners, whatever their private feelings, walked out. As Satchel Paige said, "The past is a long and twisty road."

The Southpaw

It was Warren Spahn who changed the perception that all left-handed pitchers were a little crazy.

I'm not sure where or when the idea started, but the impression was still fairly general when Spahn came along to prove that a left-hander could act in a perfectly ordinary way, except for winning twenty games every year.

No doubt, the tradition dated back to pitchers like Rube Waddell, a legend in the 1920s, who once disappeared from a game—he was the pitcher—to follow a fire truck. He was sometimes discovered between innings under the stands, shooting marbles with a bunch of kids.

Lefty Gomez came along in the 1930s to add his own touch. Gomez could throw a lot faster than he ran, but hand or foot he liked a challenge. One day George Selkirk, his Yankee teammate, anoher happy soul, said he thought he could beat Gomez to the dugout, running in from right field. They bet five dollars on it.

With two out in the next inning, and two on, the batter drove a fly ball to deep center. Gomez watched it go, saw Joe DiMaggio lope after it and then glanced toward right. Here came Selkirk, racing like a sprinter. Gomez took off for the bench, and won by a stride, just as the ball settled into the glove of Joe DiMaggio, and manager Joe McCarthy looked on in bewilderment.

Then there was Warren Spahn. No one ever suggested that Spahn had an inch of craziness in him. But anyone who played on the same team would tell you he was obsessed.

The Braves joked about it for years after manager Chuck Dressen once complained, "All he thinks about is getting his twenty."

Yet Dressen knew as well as anybody what a good thing that was for a pitcher to think about, especially one who could go out and do it. When it came to winning, Warren was selfish, and not many people begrudged him. He just didn't make it very easy on a manager. He hated to lose. Hated to get rained out. Hated to miss a turn. And hated coming out of a game with such a passion that a manager got so he dreaded going to the mound to remove him. Many of them wouldn't, and instead sent their pitching coaches. In fact, that practice may have started with Spahn.

They would practically have to Indian-wrestle with him to get the ball.

I think part of what kept that flame burning inside Spahnie was the fact that he felt he had no time to lose. He was a late starter, and he never stopped catching up.

He was forty years old my rookie season. He had just won twenty games for the thirteenth time. The *Sporting News* had voted him Pitcher of the Year.

He had signed with the Braves in 1939, years before the big bonus era, and didn't collect a dime. He spent three years in the minors and three more in the army—he was the only major-leaguer to win a battlefield commission for bravery in action.

He didn't spend a full year with the Braves until 1947, when he had the first of his twenty-game seasons (twenty-one and ten). The next year Spahn and Johnny Sain pitched the Braves to their first pennant in thirty-four years, inspiring the slogan, "Spahn and Sain and two days of rain."

I caught his record three-hundred twelfth win and he went on to add forty-one more before he retired, under protest, at the age of forty-five. His snapping fastball was gone, but he could still beat them with his off-speed pitches and his control and his head.

He was a joy to catch and a joy to watch, one of those rare people who strikes you up close just as he does from a distance. Not many ballplayers do.

Spahn moved in a peculiar sort of duck walk, his shoulders swinging from side to side, in the rambling way of a good high school athlete. His pitching form was perfect. From the side, he seemed to be turning over, automatically, like one of those old riverboat wheels, with no more strain on the arm itself than on the spoke of a wheel.

Spahnie considered himself immune to the attacks of time. When the Braves decided they needed to bring along younger pitchers, he signed on with the woeful New York Mets. He was listed as a coach, but he kept wanting to work with an old guy named Warren Spahn, rather than the bonus kids the Mets kept bringing in.

The first time he pitched against his old club in Milwaukee, the Braves scored seven runs off him in one inning, including a grand slam homer by Eddie Mathews. The fans gave Spahn a standing ovation and booed the Braves, who felt like booing themselves.

He was a grandpappy age for a pitcher, and his breaking pitches no longer dipped and wobbled like a tired moth. To Spahn it was a sad night only because he didn't win.

I have always thought that one remark typified him. The night he won his three-hundredth, he was asked what it meant, how badly he had wanted it.

He looked surprised anyone would ask. "I wanted this one," he said. "I wanted the last one, and I want the next one."

15. The All-Uke Team

I AM MORE FORTUNATE than most former big-leaguers, because I have no feelings of frustration, of promise unfulfilled. I think I got everything out of my talent I could.

To begin with, I lacked speed. I had to compensate with a few tricks. One was to knock my hat off as I ran down the first-base line, to make it appear that I was really moving.

I hated to lead off an inning, especially in a park that had Astroturf. I would hit a bouncing ball to third base and they'd whip the ball to second and then to first. It really made you look bad when they practiced their double plays with nobody on base.

The one ability I did have, and tried never to lose, was the ability to laugh at myself, or at the foibles of a game little kids play for free. After a long day, moving on to another town, the fellows usually needed some comic relief.

Once, with the Braves, we were coming in for a

landing. The time when many players tighten up is when the plane touches down, and there is this great whoosh before the brakes grab. I picked up the intercom mike in the back of the plane and announced, "This is your captain speaking. Please remain seated and keep your safety belts fastened until the plane HAS HIT THE SIDE OF THE TERMINAL BUILDING and come to a complete stop."

It was fun watching the blood leave their faces for a few seconds.

That was my way of bringing the guys together, of reminding them that man can't live by box score alone. I meant it one night, sort of, when I said on the *Tonight Show*: 'Winning and losing is nothing. Going out and prowling the streets after the game is what I liked. You'd get half in the bag and wake up the next morning with a bird in your room—that's what baseball is all about."

In that spirit, I have been persuaded to select my own All-Star team, an all-character team, composed of players whose contribution to the game went beyond winning or losing. To be eligible, their careers had to cross mine, meaning they had to have played at least one game in the National League in the years between 1961 and 1968. I gave special consideration to those whose service had a distinctive and human quality, and also to those I thought might be seriously offended by being left out. Herewith,

THE BOB UECKER ALL-STAR TEAM

FIRST BASE—*Marv Throneberry,* Mets. The competition was hotter here than at any other position, with the likes of Dick Stuart, Norm Larker and Gordy Coleman all in the running. A special honorable mention should go to Joe Pepitone, for his lasting contribution to the game. Pepitone is believed to be the first player to bring a hair blower into the locker room. Throneberry wins for a career that led not to the Hall of Fame, but to a Lite Beer commercial. He once was called out for failing to touch second base on a triple. When he complained, the umpires pointed out that he had missed first base, too.

SECOND BASE—*Rod Kanehl,* Mets. Led the league for three straight years in getting hit by pitches, and defined team spirit as being willing "to take one on the ass for the team." Once, as a pinch runner, he scored from second on a passed ball to give the Mets a 7-6 lead over the Phillies. Casey Stengel was so elated he told Hot Rod to stay in the game. When Kanehl asked which position, Casey said, "I don't care. Play any place you want to." Kanehl grabbed his glove and ran onto the field. He told Felix Mantilla to move from third to second, moved Elio Chacon from second to short, and put himself in at third. "That's the kind of ballplayers we want," Stengel said later. "Tell him to do something, and he does it."

SHORTSTOP—*Ruben Amaro,* Phillies. One of the slickest glove men ever to play the game, but I have included him for two reasons. Ruben hit even fewer homers (two) in his career than I did, and he is the only man I ever heard of who was drafted by both the American and Mexican armies. He deserves it.

THIRD BASE—*Doug Rader,* Astros. He was playing for Houston, in San Diego, the night that Padres owner Ray Kroc got on the p.a. system and apologized to the crowd for how lousy his team was. Rader rushed to the defense of the Padres, adding that Kroc "must have thought he was talking to a bunch of short-order cooks." The next week, Rader received angry letters from short-order cooks all over the country. The Padres turned the whole affair into a ticket promotion, letting in free anyone wearing a long white hat when the Astros returned to town. It all worked out swell in the off season, when Houston traded Rader to—you guessed it—San Diego.

OUTFIELD—*Roberto Clemente,* Pirates. One of the really complete players of his era, Roberto was also one of the great hypochondriacs. He suffered from insomnia, and claimed that sleeping pills kept him awake. The year he won his second batting title, he said he had gotten malaria from a mosquito, typhoid fever from a pig and food poisoning from a fish—all man's natural enemies. "I feel better when I am sick," he once said. Roberto was one beautiful wreck.

Frank Thomas, Pirates, Reds, Cubs, Mets, Phillies, Astros, Braves, etc. He played for eleven teams, three in one season. Known as the Big Donkey, partly because his bat had a kick in it (when it connected), and partly because he suffered from hoof-in-mouth disease. It seemed that every few months Thomas would be traded, always leaving with the same declaration: "It's nice to know that somebody wants you."

Frank Howard, Dodgers. It was a thrill to watch him play the outfield. Jim Murray wrote that at six-eight, Howard was the only player in baseball who clanked when he walked. Early in his career, you never knew if he would drive in more runs than he let in. He had one of the biggest swings in the game, and once took a mighty cut just as Maury Wills slid across the plate, trying to steal home. A gentle giant, Howard was more shaken than Wills. "Please, Maurice," he begged, "don't ever do that again."

PITCHERS—*Ken MacKenzie,* Mets, left-hander. The first Yale graduate I know of to pitch in the big leagues after World War II. Casey Stengel once brought him in from the bullpen to face the San Francisco Giants with the bases full. The next three hitters were Orlando Cepeda, Willie Mays and Willie McCovey. Stengel handed him the ball and said, "Pretend they are the Harvards." Another time, MacKenzie was sulking on the bench. "Do you realize," he said, "that I am the lowest-paid member of the Yale Class of '59?" Stengel reminded him, "Yes, but with the highest earned run average."

Honorable mention, *Masanori Murakami,* Giants, left-hander. There has to be a category for the only Japanese ever to pitch in the National League. Described as "sneaky fast," he compiled a 5-1 record in two seasons of relief, then returned to Japan, homesick for his native land. He spoke almost no English, but had a sense of humor. Or at least, the writers who covered the

Giants did. Asked to name his favorite American songs, Murakami replied, "Horro, Dorry," and "Up a Razy Liver."

Turk Farrell, Phillies, Dodgers, Astros, right-hander. Early in his career, as a member of the Phillies' famed Dalton Gang, he set a record for barro fights. A hard thrower, with a big follow-through, Turk later set a record for most times getting hit by batted balls on various parts of the body. A line drive by Henry Aaron once glanced off his forehead, but Farrell stayed in the game. He carried a gun in spring training one year in Arizona, and shot snakes as he walked from his hotel to the ball park. A Falstaffian figure, he beat his old club, the Phillies, in a game that went fourteen innings and ended shortly before 1:00 A.M., and boasted in the clubhouse: "Nobody beats Farrell after midnight."

Honorable mention, *Gaylord Perry*, many teams, right-hander. When he came to the big leagues, one scouting report said he was only a "marginal prospect" to stay in the majors. Twenty-two years later, he was gunning for his three hundredth win. Once, after Nellie Fox had singled in the winning run against him, Perry broke Nellie's bat at home plate. He confessed some of his other sins in a book called *Me and the Spitter*, but swore he had reformed and no longer threw the illegal pitch because he wanted to set a good example for the kids.

You may have noticed that my All-Star team has no catcher. There were several candidates for this honor. Some had talent, but their humor was just warped enough to keep them in contention, such as Tim

McCarver and Joe Torre. Others were not handicapped by their talent, such as John Bateman and Choo Choo Coleman.

In the end, I decided to leave the position vacant because I have been taught that it is in poor taste to give an award to yourself.

APPENDIX

The Record

UECKER, ROBERT GEORGE
B. Jan. 26, 1935, Milwaukee, Wisconsin
BR TR 6′1″ 190 lbs

	G	AB	H	2b	3b	HR	R	RBI	SB	BA	BB	SO
1962 MIL N	33	64	16	2	0	1	5	8	0	.250	7	15
1963	13	16	4	2	0	0	3	0	0	.250	2	5
1964 STL N	40	106	21	1	0	1	8	6	0	.198	17	24
1965	53	145	33	7	0	2	17	10	0	.228	24	27
1966 PHI N	78	207	43	6	0	7	15	30	0	.208	22	36
1967 PHI N	18									.171		
" ATL N	62									.146		
tot 2 teams	80	193	29	4	0	3	17	20	0	.150	24	60
6 years	297	731	146	22	0	14	65	74	0	.200	96	167

215

Traded to St. Louis, April 1964, for Jim Coker and Gary Kolb.

Traded to Philadelphia, January 1966, with Dick Groat and Bill White, for Alex Johnson, Pat Corrales and Art Mahaffey.

Traded to Atlanta, July 1967, for Gene Oliver.

Bestselling Books for Today's Reader